Practical Microservices with Dapr and .NET

A developer's guide to building cloud-native
applications using the Dapr event-driven runtime

Davide Bedin

BIRMINGHAM—MUMBAI

Practical Microservices with Dapr and .NET

Copyright © 2020 Packt Publishing

All rights reserved. No part of this book may be reproduced, stored in a retrieval system, or transmitted in any form or by any means, without the prior written permission of the publisher, except in the case of brief quotations embedded in critical articles or reviews.

Every effort has been made in the preparation of this book to ensure the accuracy of the information presented. However, the information contained in this book is sold without warranty, either express or implied. Neither the author, nor Packt Publishing or its dealers and distributors, will be held liable for any damages caused or alleged to have been caused directly or indirectly by this book.

Packt Publishing has endeavored to provide trademark information about all of the companies and products mentioned in this book by the appropriate use of capitals. However, Packt Publishing cannot guarantee the accuracy of this information.

Commissioning Editor: Richa Tripathi
Acquisition Editor: Karan Gupta
Senior Editor: Storm Mann
Content Development Editor: Dwayne Fernandes
Technical Editor: Pradeep Sahu
Copy Editor: Safis Editing
Project Coordinator: Deeksha Thakkar
Proofreader: Safis Editing
Indexer: Tejal Daruwale Soni
Production Designer: Roshan Kawale

First published: December 2020
Production reference: 2190121

Published by Packt Publishing Ltd.
Livery Place
35 Livery Street
Birmingham
B3 2PB, UK.

ISBN 978-1-80056-837-2

www.packt.com

To Silvia, Abramo, and Elia: nothing would have been possible without you.

– Davide Bedin

`Packt.com`

Subscribe to our online digital library for full access to over 7,000 books and videos, as well as industry leading tools to help you plan your personal development and advance your career. For more information, please visit our website.

Why subscribe?

- Spend less time learning and more time coding with practical eBooks and Videos from over 4,000 industry professionals

- Improve your learning with Skill Plans built especially for you

- Get a free eBook or video every month

- Fully searchable for easy access to vital information

- Copy and paste, print, and bookmark content

Did you know that Packt offers eBook versions of every book published, with PDF and ePub files available? You can upgrade to the eBook version at `packt.com` and as a print book customer, you are entitled to a discount on the eBook copy. Get in touch with us at `customercare@packtpub.com` for more details.

At `www.packt.com`, you can also read a collection of free technical articles, sign up for a range of free newsletters, and receive exclusive discounts and offers on Packt books and eBooks.

Foreword

A major wave of enterprise cloud adoption is underway and with this, we've seen a shift to "cloud-native" development often built with microservice architectures, both stateless and stateful, that run on the cloud and edge and that embrace the diversity of languages and frameworks available. This shift has realized massive scale and efficiency, however, it has also brought with it significant challenges, putting the burden of becoming distributed systems experts on enterprise developers and often requiring them to learn and be productive in many languages, frameworks, and technologies. There is also often the requirement for applications to be portable across the cloud and edge or across different public cloud providers. Enterprises seek to focus on business logic while leaning on platforms to imbue their applications with scale, resiliency, maintainability, elasticity, and the other attributes of cloud-native architectures.

As we observed this shift and looked to address the challenges that came with it, Dapr, which was originally called "Actions," originated as an incubation project within the Azure Office of the CTO through the creative exploration of my technical assistants, Haishi Bai and Yaron Schneider. We developed Dapr with the idea that enterprise developers building distributed systems could leverage a "butler" that would handle all the work of building distributed systems for them so they could focus on their application and business logic, hence the top hat reference in the Dapr icon. To do that we looked to build an enterprise developer-focused microservices programming model platform with the tagline "Any Language, Any Framework, Anywhere" that made building distributed applications easy and truly embraced the diversity of languages and frameworks and was portable across any infrastructure, from the public cloud through the hierarchical edge, and even down to single-node IoT devices.

To address the widest range of applications, we built upon the requirements that Actions could run across any infrastructure, including any new infrastructure platform that might emerge, including extensible systems for integration with external event sources and services, supporting any language, having built-in features of microservices architectures such as publish/subscribe and service-invocation semantics, and including both stateless and stateful microservices. As many languages and frameworks were used, we also saw the incredible value of a "butler" that can move and communicate between each of these paradigms in the same way, effectively creating a programming substrate across different ways of writing applications. This unlocked the ability for developers to easily build a microservice application with the best technology for the job, whether functions, containers, web services, and so on, and coordinate them with the common Dapr substrate using the same semantics. We publicly announced the project as Dapr with the v0.1 release in Oct 2019.

Since the initial preview, we've had an overwhelmingly positive response from the developer community, including over 500 contributions to the project external to Microsoft. We are now approaching Dapr v1.0 targeted for release in early 2021, which focuses on production readiness and moving the project toward open governance so that enterprises can be confident to bet on and leverage Dapr in business-critical workloads. We hope you will deliver more impact by focusing on your core business value and leveraging Dapr to do the rest and we are excited to have you join us on this journey as part of the Dapr community at `github.com/dapr/dapr`.

Mark Russinovich

Azure CTO and Technical Fellow

Microsoft

Contributors

About the author

Davide Bedin is a cloud-native architecture enthusiast, with strong and relevant experience with cloud platforms.

As CTO of an ISV, Davide led its significant transformational process with the objective of creating new solutions based on the Microsoft Azure cloud.

Davide particularly focused on the evolution of distributed computing to service-oriented architectures, and ultimately microservices, spending most of his developer career creating web services.

As a cloud solution architect at Microsoft, Davide is responsible for the guidance and support of enterprise customers in embracing the cloud paradigm, a key enabler of their digital transformation; lately, he also plays with Dapr.

I thank Jessica Tibaldi and Paola Annis for their precious advice in writing this book.

Also, I have been blessed with the wisdom of many great teachers during my career: there are too many to list them all here – you all know who you are.

About the reviewer

Senthil Kumar is a Microsoft MVP in Visual Studio technologies. He is a co-author of the book *Windows 10 Development Recipes Using JavaScript and CSS*, published by Apress.

Senthil has been working in the IT industry for over 9 years now and has had exposure to a variety of languages, including C#, JavaScript, PHP, and others.

Packt is searching for authors like you

If you're interested in becoming an author for Packt, please visit `authors.packtpub.com` and apply today. We have worked with thousands of developers and tech professionals, just like you, to help them share their insight with the global tech community. You can make a general application, apply for a specific hot topic that we are recruiting an author for, or submit your own idea.

Table of Contents

Section 2: Building Microservices with Dapr

3

Service-to-Service Invocation

4

Introducing State Management

5
Publish and Subscribe

6
Resource Bindings

7
Using Actors

Section 3: Deploying and Scaling Dapr Solutions

8

Deploying to Kubernetes

9

Tracing Dapr Applications

10
Load Testing and Scaling Dapr

Appendix
Microservices Architectures with Dapr

Other Books You May Enjoy

Index

Preface

Practical Microservices with Dapr and .NET helps you discover the powerful capabilities of Dapr by implementing a sample application with microservice architecture, using one of Dapr's many building blocks in each chapter of this book.

Over the last decade, there has been a huge shift from heavily coded monolithic applications to finer, self-contained microservices. Dapr is a new, open source project by Microsoft that provides proven techniques and best practices for developing modern applications. It offers platform-agnostic features for running your applications on the public cloud, on-premises, and even on edge devices.

This book aims to familiarize you with microservices architectures, while managing application complexities, and overcoming the nitty-gritty with Dapr in no time. You will also see how it combines the simplicity of implementation with its openness to multiple languages and platforms. We will explore how Dapr's runtime, services, building blocks, and SDKs will help you simplify the creation of resilient and portable microservices. Dapr provides an event-driven runtime that supports the essential features you need to build microservices, such as service invocation, state management, and publish/subscribe messaging, in addition to various other advanced features.

Dapr provides an event-driven runtime that supports the essential features you need to build microservices, such as service invocation, state management, and publish/subscribe messaging. You'll explore all of those in addition to various other advanced features with this practical guide to learning Dapr.

This book guides you in creating a sample application based on Dapr, which you'll then deploy to Kubernetes. In this operating environment, you'll learn how to monitor Dapr applications using Zipkin, Prometheus, and Grafana. Finally, you will learn how to perform load testing on Dapr applications in Kubernetes.

By the end of this book, you'll be able to write microservices easily using your choice of language or framework by implementing industry best practices to solve problems related to distributed systems.

Who this book is for

This book is for developers looking to explore microservices architectures and implement them in Dapr applications using examples on Microsoft .NET Core. Whether you are new to microservices or have knowledge of this architectural approach and want to get hands-on experience in using Dapr, you'll find this book useful. Familiarity with .NET Core will help you to understand the C# samples and code snippets used in the book.

What this book covers

Chapter 1, Introducing Dapr, introduces you to the basics of Dapr, briefly exposing the features that make Dapr interesting for new cloud-native applications as well as for inserting microservices into existing applications.

Chapter 2, Debugging Dapr Solutions, focuses on how to set up your Dapr development environment in VS Code to locally debug simple Dapr solutions as well as more complex ones.

Chapter 3, Service-to-Service Invocation, instructs you how services can discover and invoke each other via the Dapr infrastructure. With examples, you will understand how to implement services and invoke them from other Dapr-aware components and Dapr-unaware/external clients.

Chapter 4, Introducing State Management, covers a centerpiece of Dapr: the management of state for services and actors. This chapter will illustrate how a Dapr solution can manage state with different store types.

Chapter 5, Publish and Subscribe, introduces publish/subscribe – the messaging pattern used by Dapr to enable decoupled interactions between components. You will learn about the benefits of the messaging-based pattern and how to implement it in Dapr.

Chapter 6, Resource Bindings, introduces bindings in Dapr, which enable you to design event-driven microservices and to invoke external resources via a pluggable configuration.

Chapter 7, Using Actors, explains the powerful virtual actor model provided by Dapr, how to leverage it in a microservices-style architecture, and the pros and cons of different approaches.

Chapter 8, Deploying to Kubernetes, covers the basic differences in operations from local self-hosted environments to Kubernetes mode. Specifically using Azure Kubernetes Service, we will deploy a Dapr sample application composed of several microservices to Kubernetes.

Chapter 9, Tracing Dapr Applications, introduces the observability options in Dapr, by exploring how traces, logs, and metrics are emitted and can be collected in Dapr using Zipkin, Prometheus, and Grafana.

Chapter 10, Load Testing and Scaling Dapr, explains how the scaling of Dapr services and actors works in Kubernetes. Also, by leveraging autoscalers, you will learn how to scale resources based on usage metrics. You will also learn how to load test a Dapr solution by simulating user behaviors via the Locust testing tool.

Appendix, Microservices Architectures with Dapr, discusses the relevance of microservices architectures and explores how Dapr, as a runtime, can make it easier to adopt this style.

To get the most out of this book

While the samples in the book have been written on Windows 10, the technology stack used is multiplatform: VS Code, .NET Core, Dapr, Kubernetes, and Locust all offer tools and libraries for multiple platforms.

Software/hardware covered in the book
Docker Engine – the latest version
.NET Core 3.1
Dapr, release candidate 1 or later
VS Code – the latest version
Python 3.8
The Azure CLI – 2.15.1 or later
Locust 1.3.1 or later

On Windows 10, it is recommended to have WSL 2 installed and enable the WSL 2 engine in Docker.

For detailed instructions on how to set up your environment, please see the *Setting up Dapr* section in *Chapter 1, Introducing Dapr*.

If you are using the digital version of this book, we advise you to type the code yourself or access the code via the GitHub repository (link available in the next section). Doing so will help you avoid any potential errors related to the copying and pasting of code.

The Dapr runtime is getting closer to being released as the v1.0 production-ready version.

*The samples and scripts in this book have been tested with the first **release candidate (RC)** of Dapr, version v1.0.0.0-rc.1.*

Download the example code files

You can download the example code files for this book from GitHub at `https://github.com/PacktPublishing/Practical-Microservices-with-Dapr-and-.NET`. In case there's an update to the code, it will be updated on the existing GitHub repository.

We also have other code bundles from our rich catalog of books and videos available at `https://github.com/PacktPublishing/`. Check them out!

Download the color images

We also provide a PDF file that has color images of the screenshots/diagrams used in this book. You can download it here: `https://static.packt-cdn.com/downloads/9781800568372_ColorImages.pdf`.

Conventions used

There are a number of text conventions used throughout this book.

`Code in text`: Indicates code words in text, database table names, folder names, filenames, file extensions, pathnames, dummy URLs, user input, and Twitter handles. Here is an example: "All we need to do is refer to the previously defined configurations in `launch.json`."

A block of code is set as follows:

```
"compounds":
    [
        {
            "name": "webApi + webApi2 w/Dapr",
            "configurations": [".NET Core Launch w/Dapr (webapi)",
            ".NET Core Launch w/Dapr (webapi2)"]
        }
    ]
```

When we wish to draw your attention to a particular part of a code block, the relevant lines or items are set in bold:

```
{
        "appId": "hello-world",
        "appPort": 5000,
        "httpPort": 5010,
        "grpcPort": 50010,
        "label": "daprd-debug",
        "type": "daprd",
        "dependsOn": "build"
    }
```

Any command-line input or output is written as follows:

```
$ mkdir css
$ cd css
```

Bold: Indicates a new term, an important word, or words that you see onscreen. For example, words in menus or dialog boxes appear in the text like this. Here is an example: "Select **System info** from the **Administration** panel."

> **Tips or important notes**
> Appear like this.

Get in touch

Feedback from our readers is always welcome.

General feedback: If you have questions about any aspect of this book, mention the book title in the subject of your message and email us at customercare@packtpub.com.

Errata: Although we have taken every care to ensure the accuracy of our content, mistakes do happen. If you have found a mistake in this book, we would be grateful if you would report this to us. Please visit www.packtpub.com/support/errata, selecting your book, clicking on the Errata Submission Form link, and entering the details.

Piracy: If you come across any illegal copies of our works in any form on the Internet, we would be grateful if you would provide us with the location address or website name. Please contact us at copyright@packt.com with a link to the material.

If you are interested in becoming an author: If there is a topic that you have expertise in and you are interested in either writing or contributing to a book, please visit `authors.packtpub.com`.

Reviews

Please leave a review. Once you have read and used this book, why not leave a review on the site that you purchased it from? Potential readers can then see and use your unbiased opinion to make purchase decisions, we at Packt can understand what you think about our products, and our authors can see your feedback on their book. Thank you!

For more information about Packt, please visit `packt.com`.

Section 1: Introduction to Dapr

This first part of the book will give you a starting point for Dapr, with an overview of what it is and its main features and components.

This section has the following chapters:

- *Chapter 1, Introducing Dapr*
- *Chapter 2, Debugging Dapr Solutions*

1
Introducing Dapr

This chapter will introduce you to the **Distributed Application Runtime (Dapr)** project to teach you the core concepts of its architecture and prepare you to develop with Dapr.

Dapr accelerates the development of new cloud-native applications and simplifies the adoption of microservice architecture.

In this chapter, we are going to cover the following main topics:

- An overview of Dapr
- The architecture of Dapr
- Setting up Dapr
- Building our first Dapr sample

At this stage, learning these topics is important with regard to obtaining a solid foundation on Dapr internals and understanding its approach to microservices architecture. These basic concepts will guide our learning throughout the rest of this book.

Our first steps into the project will start with exploring Dapr and understanding how it works.

Technical requirements

The code for this sample can be found in GitHub at `https://github.com/PacktPublishing/Practical-Microservices-with-Dapr-and-.NET/tree/main/chapter01`.

In this chapter, the working area for scripts and code is expected to be `<repository path>\chapter01\`. In my local environment, it is `C:\Repos\dapr-samples\chapter01`.

Please refer to the section *Setting up Dapr* for a complete guide on the tools needed to develop with Dapr and work with the samples.

An overview of Dapr

Dapr is an **event-driven**, **portable** runtime, created by Microsoft with an open source approach and, at the time of writing this book, still in active development.

Being event-driven, which is emphasized in the definition of Dapr, plays an important role in microservices as the application can be designed to efficiently react to events, from external systems or other parts of the solution, and to produce events as well, in order to inform other services of new facts or to continue processing elsewhere or at a later stage.

Dapr is portable as it can run locally on your development machine in self-hosted mode, it can be deployed to the edge, or it can run on Kubernetes.

The following diagram shows the many building blocks of Dapr architecture:

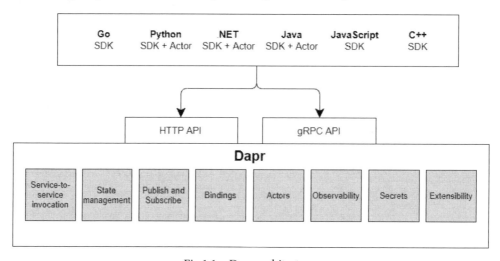

Fig 1.1 – Dapr architecture

Portability does also extend beyond the hosting environment – while Dapr is an initiative started by Microsoft, it can also run on Kubernetes on-premise or in the cloud: Microsoft Azure, Amazon AWS, Google GCP, or any other cloud vendor.

Dapr has been built on the experiences gained by Microsoft in developing hyperscale cloud-native applications. It has been inspired by the design of Orleans and Service Fabric, which in turn enable many Microsoft Azure cloud services to operate resiliently and at large scale.

Dapr offers developers an approach to design, the tools to build, and the runtime to operate applications based on the microservices architecture style.

Microservices offer a vast array of benefits balanced by increased complexities in team and product management, usually with a significant burden on the developer and the team in order to get started.

What if you could leverage a runtime such as Dapr to help you get through the common patterns you will likely need to adopt and ease your operations?

This diagram shows the two Dapr hosting modes:

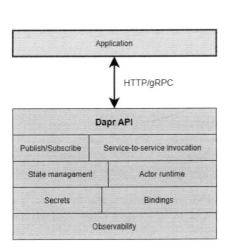 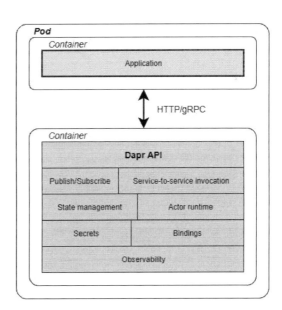

Fig 1.2. Dapr sidecar

As depicted in *Figure 1.2*, the Dapr runtime operates in sidecar processes, lifting most of the complexity from the application to a separate environment, greatly simplifying development and operations as well. These sidecar processes are run locally in your development environment or as containers in a Pod on Kubernetes.

From the application perspective, Dapr is an API that can be directly reached via HTTP or gRPC calls or, even more simply, via any of the SDKs available. At the time of writing this book, these are .NET Core, Java, Go, Python, C++, JavaScript, and Rust.

As we will experience later, it is not necessary to adopt the Dapr SDK in your application: a call to a Dapr service can be as simple as an HTTP call to an endpoint such as `http://localhost:3500/v1.0/invoke/<app-id>/method/<method name>`. Nevertheless, using the SDK does provide many benefits if you are writing a Dapr service or leveraging the Dapr actor model.

What Dapr is not

While I hope the overview of Dapr informed and intrigued you enough to spend your time on this book, when I have the chance to talk about Dapr, I often find myself in need of clarifying what Dapr is *not*. This makes it easier to eliminate any misconceptions we may have about what Dapr does:

- Dapr's goal is *not* to force the developer to embrace a programming model with strict rules and constraints. On the contrary, while the application developer is freed by Dapr of the many complexities of a microservice architecture, the developer is not mandated on how to write the application. As an example, the management of the connection pooling to the database where the state is stored is a responsibility of Dapr and, as we will see in the following chapters, it is transparent to the microservice application code.

- Dapr is *not* a service mesh. While many similarities can be found in the general objectives of Dapr and service meshes, Dapr does provide these benefits at the application level while a service mesh operates on the infrastructure. For instance, Dapr applies retry logic in its interaction with state stores and services, but it is the developer's responsibility to decide how to handle the error Dapr might return if there is a conflict or an intermittent issue: whether raising the error back to the client, compensating the operation, or adopting a retry policy (maybe leveraging Polly in .NET Core) – it is an explicit choice only the developer can make.
  Dapr is meant to be integrated with service meshes, such as Istio, which is out of the scope of this book.

- Dapr is *not* a Microsoft cloud service: it does help the developer build microservice applications in the cloud, and it surely provides many integrations with Azure cloud services, but it also has as many components for AWS, GCP, and other services.

  It is also true that Dapr does not run on Azure better than on any other Kubernetes environment in the cloud. I would like to convince you that Azure Kubernetes Service is the best managed Kubernetes offering in the cloud space, but this is a different conversation for another time.

> **Important note**
> While this book is heavily skewed toward .NET Core, Dapr does provide the same benefits to Python (just as an example) developers, as it provides SDKs for Dapr and Dapr actor, working on macOS and with Kubernetes as the deployment target: Dapr welcomes all developers in a vendor-neutral and open approach.

The next section will be dedicated to understanding the architectures that Dapr can enable.

The architecture of Dapr

Dapr has been designed from the ground up as a set of pluggable building blocks: developers can create an application counting on the support of many facilities while operators can adapt applications to the hosting environment by simply intervening in the configuration.

The following is a complete list of the tools and components of Dapr:

- **The Dapr CLI**: A cross-platform command-line tool to configure, manage, and monitor the Dapr environment. It is also the tool to locally debug Dapr applications.

- **The Dapr API**: The API that defines how an application can interact with the Dapr runtime in order to leverage its building blocks.

- **The Dapr runtime**: This is the core of Dapr, which implements the API. If you are curious, you can take a look at how it is developed in Go at Dapr's repository: `https://github.com/dapr/dapr`.

- **The Dapr host**: On your development machine, the host runs as a standalone process; in Kubernetes, it is a sidecar container in your application's pod.

- **The Dapr operator**: Specific to Kubernetes mode, the operator manages bindings and configurations.

- **The Dapr sidecar injector**: Once instructed via configuration in Kubernetes mode, it takes care of injecting the Dapr sidecar into your application pod.

- **The Dapr placement service**: This service has the objective of distributing (or placing) actor instances across the Dapr pods.

- **Dapr Sentry**: A built-in certificate authority to issue and manage certificates used by Dapr to provide transparent mTLS.

Dapr provides several building blocks that microservice application developers can adopt selectively, based on their needs:

- **Service invocation**: Service-to-service invocation enables your code to call other services located in the same hosting environment while taking care of the retry policy.

  This building block is presented in more detail in *Chapter 3, Service-to-Service Invocation*.

- **State management**: This is to efficiently manage the application state as a simple key/value pair, relieving your stateful or stateless services of the need to support different backends. Dapr provides many state stores, which include Redis, Azure CosmosDB, Azure SQL Server, PostgreSQL, which can be plugged in via configuration.

  You can learn about this building block in *Chapter 4, Introducing State Management*.

- **Publish and subscribe messaging**: The publish/subscribe pattern enables decoupled communication between microservices by exchanging messages, counting on the presence of a service bus, which can route messages between producers and consumers.

  A discussion of this building block is presented in *Chapter 5, Publish and Subscribe*.

- **Resource bindings**: This is where the event-driven nature of Dapr shines: with bindings, your application can be triggered by an SMS sent via Twilio (just to name a popular service in this area).

  This building block is presented in more detail in *Chapter 6, Resource Bindings*.

- **Actors**: The actor pattern aims to simplify highly concurrent scenarios by splitting the overall requests load between a large number of computation units (the actors), which take care of the job in their smaller, but independent, scope by processing requests to a single actor one at a time: Dapr provides great benefits in this space.

You can learn about this building block in *Chapter 7, Using Actors.*

- **Observability**: Dapr enables the developer and operator to observe the behavior of the system services and applications without having to instrument them.

  This building block is presented in more detail in *Chapter 9, Tracing Dapr Applications.*

- **Secrets**: It is a common requirement and a healthy practice to keep secrets at a safe distance from the code, even if only to prevent unintended access in a development environment to the connection string intended for the production environment. Dapr enables you to store secrets and to reference these from other Dapr components, in Kubernetes or Azure Key Vault, among many options.

After learning about Dapr architecture and components, and before we can start using them, we need to set up Dapr in our development environment, which will be the topic of the next section.

Setting up Dapr

Dapr is a runtime for every platform and every language. The focus of this book is on C# in .NET Core, used from Visual Studio Code. The code snippets in the book can be appreciated by developers from any background, but nevertheless, you will get the most out of it from the .NET Core perspective.

The development environment I use is Windows 10, as you will be able to tell from the screenshots we use in the book. While the CLI, configuration, and files will be the same, if you need more details on how to perform a particular action on Linux or a macOS development machine, I encourage you to check the Dapr documentation at `https://docs.dapr.io/`.

> **Important note: roadmap to v1.0**
>
> The Dapr runtime is getting closer to being released as the v1.0 production-ready version.
>
> The samples and scripts in this book have been tested with the first release candidate (RC) of Dapr, version v1.0.0.0-rc.1.

Docker

Dapr requires Docker locally on your development environment, therefore make sure you have it installed. If your development machine is Windows, Docker must be running in Linux containers mode.

You can find detailed instructions for running Docker at `https://docs.docker.com/install/`.

The Dapr CLI

We will immediately start working with Dapr; therefore, you need to install all the necessary tools. The Dapr runtime and its tools can be found at `https://github.com/dapr/cli`.

On Windows, it is suggested to use the following command to install the CLI in the `%USERPROFILE%\.dapr\` folder and add it to the user `PATH` environment variable so the tools can be found from the command line:

```
powershell -Command "$script=iwr -useb https://raw.
githubusercontent.com/dapr/cli/master/install/install.
ps1; $block=[ScriptBlock]::Create($script); invoke-command
-ScriptBlock $block -ArgumentList 1.0.0-rc.2"
```

The previous command installs a release candidate version of the Dapr CLI. Please refer to `https://docs.dapr.io/getting-started/install-dapr-cli/` for details.

We still need to initialize Dapr on the development machine, which we will do later in this chapter.

.NET Core

To install .NET Core, please refer to `https://dotnet.microsoft.com/download` for the link to the latest binaries.

On a development machine, it makes sense to install the full SDK, which includes the runtime. Once the install is complete, open a new Command Prompt and run the command `dotnet --info`. You should see the following output:

```
PS C:\Repos\dapr-samples\chapter01> dotnet --info
.NET Core SDK (reflecting any global.json):
 Version:   3.1.200
 Commit:    c5123d973b

Runtime Environment:
```

```
OS Name:      Windows
OS Version:   10.0.19041
OS Platform:  Windows
RID:          win10-x64
Base Path:    C:\Program Files\dotnet\sdk\3.1.200\
...
```

This proves dotnet has been recognized and the framework is working fine.

Visual Studio Code

Visual Studio Code (also referred to as VS Code throughout the book) is a great multiplatform source code editor by Microsoft. You can install it for free by following the instructions at `https://code.visualstudio.com/docs/setup/windows`.

The Dapr extension

Dapr has an extension for Visual Studio Code that helps with navigating the Dapr local environment and eases the debugging configuration – I highly recommend it. Please follow the instructions at `https://docs.dapr.io/developing-applications/ides/vscode/`.

Windows Terminal

I really love the new Windows Terminal (`https://aka.ms/terminal`) for its ease of use and configurability. In the following chapters, we will often have to run multiple commands and tools in parallel. Therefore, the tabs feature of Windows Terminal is just one of the reasons why I suggest you adopt it too.

Installing self-hosted Dapr

Dapr can be initialized in two modes: **self-hosted** (or standalone) and **Kubernetes**.

As it is intended to be used only for a development environment, the self-hosted mode locally installs Redis, the Dapr placement services, and Zipkin. The following command initializes Dapr on your local environment:

```
dapr init
```

In a local development environment, it might happen that the ports Dapr intends to use for Redis, for example, are already in use. In this case, you should identify which processes or containers are using the ports and change it accordingly.

Once you launch the `init`, this is the output you should expect:

```
PS C:\dapr> dapr init
Making the jump to hyperspace...
Downloading binaries and setting up components...
Downloaded binaries and completed components set up.
daprd binary has been installed to C:\Users\dabedin\.dapr\bin.
dapr_placement container is running.
dapr_redis container is running.
dapr_zipkin container is running.
Use `docker ps` to check running containers.
Success! Dapr is up and running. To get started, go here:
https://aka.ms/dapr-getting-started
```

To check your newly initialized Dapr environment, you can use `docker ps`:

```
PS C:\dapr> docker ps --format "{{.ID}}: {{.Image}} -
{{.Ports}} - {{.Names}}"
2082b7f0eda4: daprio/dapr - 0.0.0.0:6050->50005/tcp - dapr_
placement
6c68d869cea7: redis - 0.0.0.0:6379->6379/tcp - dapr_redis
e4c8eae6992d: openzipkin/zipkin - 9410/tcp, 0.0.0.0:9411->9411/
tcp - dapr_zipkin
```

The output shows the Docker container running on my machine.

Installing Dapr in Kubernetes

Dapr is specifically intended to be executed on Kubernetes. From your development machine, on which you have the Dapr CLI installed, you can set up Dapr on the Kubernetes cluster currently configured:

```
dapr init -k
```

Alternatively, you can install Dapr on Kubernetes with a Helm v3 chart. You can find more details at `https://docs.dapr.io/getting-started/install-dapr-kubernetes/#install-with-helm-advanced`.

> **Important note**
> If you intend to define a CI/CD pipeline that takes care of the Dapr installation on the Kubernetes cluster too, this can also work, although it is out of scope for the present setup.

To verify the installation completed successfully, execute this command:

```
kubectl get pods --namespace dapr-system
```

The command should display the pods in the `dapr-system` namespace.

Updating the Dapr version

On a development Windows machine, on which a previous version of Dapr was already present, this is the output of an update of the CLI:

```
powershell -Command "$script=iwr -useb https://raw.
githubusercontent.com/dapr/cli/master/install/install.
ps1; $block=[ScriptBlock]::Create($script); invoke-command
-ScriptBlock $block -ArgumentList 1.0.0-rc.2"

WARNING: Dapr is detected - c:\dapr\dapr.exe
CLI version: 0.11.0
Runtime version: n/a
Reinstalling Dapr...
Creating c:\dapr directory
Downloading https://github.com/dapr/cli/releases/download/
v1.0.0-rc.2/dapr_windows_amd64.zip ...
Extracting c:\dapr\dapr_windows_amd64.zip...
CLI version: 1.0.0-rc.2
Runtime version: n/a
Clean up c:\dapr\dapr_windows_amd64.zip...
Try to add c:\dapr to User Path Environment variable...
Skipping to add c:\dapr to User Path - … omitted …

Dapr CLI is installed successfully.
To get started with Dapr, please visit https://docs.dapr.io/
getting-started/ .
Ensure that Docker Desktop is set to Linux containers mode when
you run Dapr in self hosted mode.
```

The process to update the Dapr runtime is similar to the initialization, but first, we will need to uninstall Dapr from your machine:

```
PS C:\dapr> dapr uninstall
Removing Dapr from your machine...
Removing directory: C...
Removing container: dapr_placement
Dapr has been removed successfully
```

After we execute dapr init, if we check the Dapr version, we can see it is now moved forward from 0.8.0 to 0.10.0 for both the CLI and the runtime:

```
PS C:\dapr> dapr --version
CLI version: 1.0.0-rc.2
Runtime version: 1.0.0-rc.1
```

Our Dapr test environment is up and running: we are now ready to try it with the first sample.

Building our first Dapr example

It is time to see Dapr in action: we are going to build a web API that returns a *hello world* message. I chose to base all my samples in the C:\Repos\dapr-samples\ folder, and I created a C:\Repos\dapr-samples\chapter01 folder for this first example:

1. Let's start by creating a WebAPI .NET Core project:

    ```
    PS C:\Repos\dapr-samples\chapter01> dotnet new webapi -o
    dapr.microservice.webapi
    ```

2. Then we add the reference to the Dapr SDK for ASP.NET Core. The current version is 0.12.0-preview01. You can look for the package versions on NuGet at https://www.nuget.org/packages/Dapr.Actors.AspNetCore/ with the dotnet add package command:

    ```
    PS C:\Repos\dapr-samples\chapter01> dotnet add package
    Dapr.AspNetCore --version 0.12.0-preview01
    ```

3. We need to apply some changes to the template we used to create the project. These are going to be much easier to do via VS Code, with the <directory>\code. command We open it in the scope of the project folder.

4. To support Dapr in ASP.NET Core, I made a few changes to the code. In
    `Startup.cs`, I changed the method `ConfigureServices` to `services.`
    `AddControllers().AddDapr();`.

In `Configure`, I also added `endpoints.MapSubscribeHandler();`. This
is not necessary for this sample as we will not use the pub/sub features of Dapr.
Nevertheless, it is better to have it in mind as the base set of changes you need to
apply to a default ASP.NET project.

Finally, in order to simplify the code, I removed `app.`
`UseHttpsRedirection();`.

The following is the modified code of the `Startup.cs` class:

```
using System;
using System.Collections.Generic;
using System.Linq;
using System.Threading.Tasks;
using Microsoft.AspNetCore.Builder;
using Microsoft.AspNetCore.Hosting;
using Microsoft.AspNetCore.HttpsPolicy;
using Microsoft.AspNetCore.Mvc;
using Microsoft.Extensions.Configuration;
using Microsoft.Extensions.DependencyInjection;
using Microsoft.Extensions.Hosting;
using Microsoft.Extensions.Logging;

namespace dapr.microservice.webapi
{
    public class Startup
    {
        public Startup(IConfiguration configuration)
        {
            Configuration = configuration;
        }
        public IConfiguration Configuration { get; }

        // This method gets called by the runtime. Use
            this method to add services to the container.
        public void ConfigureServices(IServiceCollection
        services)
        {
            services.AddControllers().AddDapr();
        }
```

```
        // This method gets called by the runtime. Use
            this method to configure the HTTP request
            pipeline.
        public void Configure(IApplicationBuilder app,
        IWebHostEnvironment env)
        {
            if (env.IsDevelopment())
            {
                app.UseDeveloperExceptionPage();
            }

            app.UseRouting();

            app.UseAuthorization();

            app.UseEndpoints(endpoints =>
            {
                endpoints.MapSubscribeHandler();
                endpoints.MapControllers();
            });
        }
    }
}
```

In the preceding code, I instructed Dapr to leverage the MVC pattern in ASP.NET
Core. Keep in mind there is an alternate approach for Dapr in ASP.NET Core, which
does rely on ASP.NET Core routing with MapGet(...) and MapPost(...).
You can see an example at https://github.com/dapr/dotnet-sdk/tree/
master/samples/AspNetCore/RoutingSample.

5. Finally, I added a controller named HelloWorldController:

```
using Dapr;
using Microsoft.AspNetCore.Mvc;
using System;

namespace dapr.microservice.webapi.Controllers
{
    [ApiController]
    public class HelloWorldController : ControllerBase
    {
        [HttpGet("hello")]
        public ActionResult<string> Get()
        {
            Console.WriteLine("Hello, World.");
```

```
            return "Hello, World";
        }
    }
}
```

In the preceding code, you can see [HttpGet ("hello")]: this ASP.NET Core attribute is evaluated by Dapr to identify the method name.

6. In order to run a Dapr application, you use the following format:

```
dapr run -app-id <your app id> --app-port <port of the
application> --dapr-http-port <port in Dapr> dotnet run
```

I left the ASP.NET Core default port 5000 but I changed the Dapr HTTP port to 5010. The following command line launches the Dapr application:

```
PS C:\Repos\dapr-samples\chapter01\dapr.microservice.webapi>
dapr run --app-id hello-world --app-port 5000 --dapr-http-port
5010 dotnet run
Starting Dapr with id hello-world. HTTP Port: 5010. gRPC Port:
52443
```

The initial message informs you that Dapr is going to use port 5010 for HTTP as specified, while for gRPC it is going to auto-select an available port.

The log from Dapr is full of information. To confirm your application is running correctly in the context of the Dapr runtime, you can look for this part:

```
Updating metadata for app command: dotnet run
You're up and running! Both Dapr and your app logs will
appear here.
```

At this stage, ASP.NET Core is responding locally on port 5000 and Dapr is responding on 5010. In order to test Dapr, let's invoke a curl command. Using the browser is equally fine:

```
PS C:\Windows\System32> curl http://localhost:5010/v1.0/
invoke/hello-world/method/hello
Hello, World
```

This exciting response has been returned by Dapr, which passed our (the client's) initial request to the ASP.NET Core Web API. You should also see it logged, as Console. WriteLine sends its output to the Dapr window:

```
== APP == Hello, World.
```

7. From another window, let's verify our Dapr service details: instead of using the
    `dapr list` command, let's open the Dapr dashboard:

```
PS C:\Windows\System32> dapr dashboard
Dapr Dashboard running on http://localhost:8080
```

We can open the dashboard by navigating to `http://localhost:8080`:

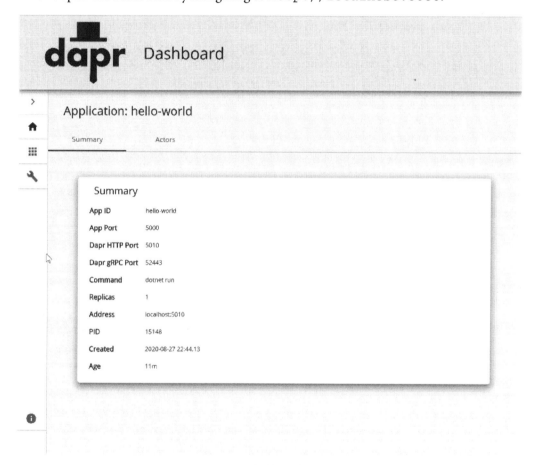

Fig. 1.3 – Dapr dashboard application

The Dapr dashboard shown in the figure illustrates the details of our `hello-world` application.

In this case, the Dapr dashboard shows only this sample application we are running on the development machine. In a Kubernetes environment, it would show all the microservices running and the other components.

The Dapr dashboard also displays the configured components in the hosting environment:

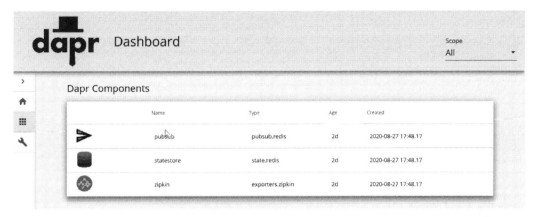

Fig. 1.4 – Dapr dashboard components

In *Figure 1.4*, the Dapr dashboard shows us that the local installation of Redis is configured as state store and pub/sub components, in addition to the deployment of Zipkin.

This ends our introductory section where we were able to build our first Dapr sample.

Summary

In this chapter, you have learned about the Distributed Application Runtime project, with its components, building blocks, and the sidecar approach. All of these concepts will be explored individually in further depth in the following chapters. You are now able to set up Dapr on your local development machine and prepare all the necessary tools to make this experience easier.

You have also learned how to create a simple ASP.NET Core project, how to configure and check Dapr, and we have had a glimpse of the Dapr dashboard to gain a complete and immediate view of the Dapr environment.

In the next chapter, we will use the newly created environment to learn how to debug Dapr.

2
Debugging Dapr Solutions

In this chapter, you will learn how to set up your local development environment in Visual Studio Code to locally debug simple Dapr solutions, as well as more complex ones.

The base concepts of Dapr execution are presented with several different approaches: via the CLI, a VS Code debug session, and Tye. Depending on your preferences, you will choose the one that suits you most and adopt it throughout the rest of the book.

These are the objectives of this chapter:

- Configuring Dapr debug in VS Code
- Debugging a Dapr multi-project solution
- Using Tye with Dapr

In learning, there is no substitute for practice: Dapr is no exception, and to practice it we will often resort to launching one Dapr application (or many) to investigate how it behaves – the sooner we are able to debug it, the better. We will start by configuring VS Code.

Technical requirements

The code for this sample can be found on GitHub at `https://github.com/PacktPublishing/Practical-Microservices-with-Dapr-and-.NET/tree/main/chapter02`.

In this chapter, the working area for scripts and code is expected to be `<repository path>\chapter02\`. In my local environment, it is `C:\Repos\dapr-samples\chapter02`.

Please refer to the section *Setting up Dapr* in *Chapter 1*, *Introducing Dapr*, for a complete guide on the tools needed to develop with Dapr and work with the samples.

Configuring Dapr debug in VS Code

Over the course of this book, we will leverage **Visual Studio Code** (**VS Code**) in exploring Dapr via several examples. Before we delve into the detailed features of Dapr, we need to understand how the multi-platform code editor VS Code can be configured to help us debug our sample code.

For an extended guide on how to set up Dapr debugging in VS Code, see the documentation at `https://docs.dapr.io/developing-applications/ides/vscode/#manually-configuring-visual-studio-code-for-debugging-with-daprd`.

The following steps will guide us in configuring debugging in VS Code on a copy of our *hello world* sample from the previous chapter.

Attaching the debugger

In the working area, you will find the samples from *Chapter 1*, *Introducing Dapr*. From Command Prompt, you can launch the sample via the Dapr CLI with the command `dotnet run` to launch the Web API, previously modified to accommodate Dapr:

```
PS C:\Repos\dapr-samples\chapter02\sample.microservice.webapi>
dapr run --app-id hello-world --app-port 5000 --dapr-http-port
5010 dotnet run
```

You should expect this output:

```
Starting Dapr with id hello-world. HTTP Port: 5010. gRPC Port:
57138
...
Updating metadata for app command: dotnet run
```

```
You're up and running! Both Dapr and your app logs will appear
here.
```

Without any additional configuration, other than the default provided by VS Code, we can attach the .NET running code to debug our Dapr sample service.

As we are going to change the debug configurations later, I suggest that we grow accustomed to it.

The following is the default content of the `launch.json` file for a .NET Web API project – at this stage, we will focus on the *.NET Core Attach* config:

```
{
    "version": "0.2.0",
    "configurations": [
        {
            "name": ".NET Core Launch (web)",
            "type": "coreclr",
            "request": "launch",
            "preLaunchTask": "build",
            //
            "program": "${workspaceFolder}/bin/Debug/
netcoreapp3.1/sample.microservice.webapi.dll",
            "args": [],
            "cwd": "${workspaceFolder}",
            "stopAtEntry": false,
            // Enable launching a web browser when ASP.NET
            Core starts. For more information: https://aka.ms/
            VSCode-CS-LaunchJson-WebBrowser
            "serverReadyAction": {
                "action": "openExternally",
                "pattern": "\\bNow listening on:\\
                    s+(https?://\\S+)"
            },
            "env": {
                "ASPNETCORE_ENVIRONMENT": "Development"
            },
            "sourceFileMap": {
                "/Views": "${workspaceFolder}/Views"
            }
        },
        {
            "name": ".NET Core Attach",
            "type": "coreclr",
            "request": "attach",
```

```
                    "processId": "${command:pickProcess}"
        }
    ]
}
```

In the preceding configuration, there is nothing special other than asking the end user which process to attach the VS Code debugging experience to.

With our Dapr `hello-world` service running in a Dapr runtime process (`daprd.exe`) launched via the Dapr CLI, by starting the VS Code debugging configuration named *.NET Core Attach*, we should look for the .NET Web API server process instead. In this context, it can be found as `sample.microservice.webapi.exe`, as you can see from the following screenshot:

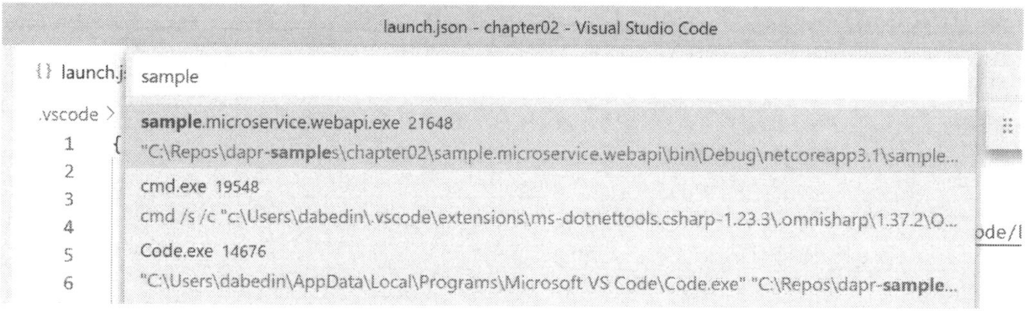

Figure 2.1 – Attach debug to process in VS Code

Once we have selected the right process to attach the debugger to, we should be able to set breakpoints in VS Code and properly debug our code.

This was an easy approach to start with, although it might prove less than optimal with frequent debugging or more complex projects. Next, we'll examine the configuration in more detail.

Examining the debug configuration

The next objective is to instruct our VS Code to combine both steps: launching Dapr via the CLI and attaching the debugger.

> **TIP**
>
> You can activate the command palette in VS Code with the *Ctrl + Shift + P* keys. For more details on the tool's user interface, see https://code.visualstudio.com/docs/getstarted/userinterface.

Instead of manually configuring `launch.json`, we can leverage the Dapr extension for VS Code to scaffold the configuration for us.

In our *hello-world* sample, let's open the command palette and look for Dapr tasks. Among these, we can find **Dapr: Scaffold Dapr Tasks**:

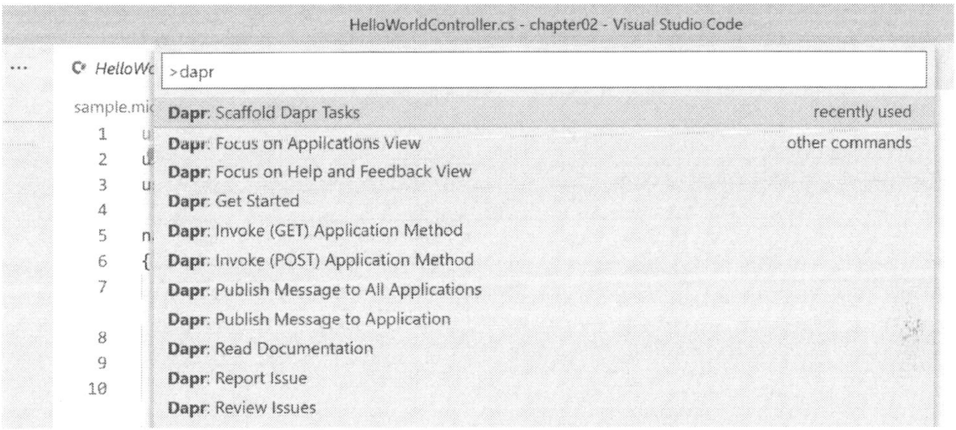

Figure 2.2 – Tasks in the Dapr extension for VS Code

By selecting it, we get asked which launch base configuration to derive from: the default **.NET Core Launch (web)** is the one to choose.

To stay consistent with our direct usage of the Dapr CLI, we set `hello-world` as the App ID and leave the default `app-port 5000`. The following extract of `launch.json` displays the relevant changes:

```
{
    "version": "0.2.0",
    "configurations": [
        {
            "name": ".NET Core Launch (web)",
            ... omitted ...
        },
        {
            "name": ".NET Core Attach",
            ... omitted ...
        },
        {

            "name": ".NET Core Launch (web) with Dapr",
            "type": "coreclr",
            "request": "launch",
            "preLaunchTask": "daprd-debug",
```

```
            "program": "${workspaceFolder}/bin/Debug/netcoreapp3.1/
            sample.microservice.webapi.dll",
            "args": [],
            "cwd": "${workspaceFolder}",
            "stopAtEntry": false,
            "serverReadyAction": {
                "action": "openExternally",
                "pattern": "\\bNow listening on:\\s+(https?://\\
                S+)"
            },
            "env": {
                "ASPNETCORE_ENVIRONMENT": "Development"
            },
            "sourceFileMap": {
                "/Views": "${workspaceFolder}/Views"
            },
            "postDebugTask": "daprd-down"
        }
    ]
}
```

The `tasks.json` file has also been prepared by the Dapr extension task:

```
{
    "version": "2.0.0",
    "tasks": [
        … omitted …
        {
            "appId": "hello-world",
            "appPort": 5000,
            "label": "daprd-debug",
            "type": "daprd",
            "dependsOn": "build"
        },
        {
            "appId": "hello-world",
            "label": "daprd-down",
            "type": "daprd-down"
        }
    ]
}
```

Once we activate debugging in VS Code by selecting the **.NET Core Launch (web) with Dapr** configuration, this is what happens, in order:

1. The `"daprd-debug"` task is invoked.

2. This task has a dependency on the `"build"` task, which, as the name implies, builds the .NET project.

3. The newly built .NET Web API is executed.

4. The task has the type `"daprd"`: the Dapr debugger is invoked with the configured settings.

5. Once we are done with debugging, the `"dapr-down"` task is invoked to stop the Dapr service.

> TIP
>
> Keep in mind, the VS Code debug configuration is an alternative approach to launching via the Dapr CLI: on a development environment, you cannot have multiple processes trying to run the same application ID with port numbers already in use.

I recommend that you explicitly edit the task in `task.json` to accommodate for the local development environment needs. To match the Dapr CLI syntax `dapr run --app-id hello-world --app-port 5000 --dapr-http-port 5010 dotnet run` we've used so far, `appPort` is the port used by the .NET Web API application, while `httpPort` and `grpcPort` are configured to expose Dapr endpoints:

```
{
            "appId": "hello-world",
            "appPort": 5000,
            "httpPort": 5010,
            "grpcPort": 50010,
            "label": "daprd-debug",
            "type": "daprd",
            "dependsOn": "build"
}
```

If we launch the VS Code debug configuration, the following is the terminal output, showing the expected steps:

```
> Executing task: C:\Program Files\dotnet\dotnet.exe build C:\
Repos\dapr-samples\chapter02\sample.microservice.webapi/sample.
microservice.webapi.csproj /property:GenerateFullPaths=true /
consoleloggerparameters:NoSummary <
```

```
Microsoft (R) Build Engine version 16.5.0+d4cbfca49 for .NET
Core
Copyright (C) Microsoft Corporation. All rights reserved.
   Restore completed in 49,91 ms for C:\Repos\dapr-samples\
chapter02\sample.microservice.webapi\sample.microservice.
webapi.csproj.
   sample.microservice.webapi -> C:\Repos\dapr-samples\
chapter02\sample.microservice.webapi\bin\Debug\netcoreapp3.1\
sample.microservice.webapi.dll
Terminal will be reused by tasks, press any key to close it.
> Executing task: daprd-debug <
> Executing command: daprd --app-id "hello-world" --app-port
"5000" --dapr-grpc-port "50010" --dapr-http-port "5010"
--placement-address "localhost:50005" <
```

The latest command shows how the debug configuration is leveraging the Dapr CLI with the exact ports and settings we specified for `task.json`.

By reaching Dapr at the URL `http://localhost:5010/v1.0/invoke/hello-world/method/hello`, we received the expected results, this time in an integrated debugging experience inside of VS Code.

We have successfully configured VS Code to be able to rapidly build our .NET project, start Dapr with our configuration, and clean up at the end. We'll do all that in the coming sections.

Debugging a Dapr multi-project solution

In this section, we will configure debugging for multiple ASP.NET projects. In most cases, a .NET solution is developed in different projects, each representing a microservice or another component of the overall architecture. This is even more true in Dapr, which emphasizes and facilitates the development of microservices.

In this context, we leverage the VS Code capability to debug multiple projects at once. For more details, see the documentation at `https://code.visualstudio.com/docs/editor/debugging#_multitarget-debugging`.

Previously, with only one project we needed to launch, we leveraged the *Scaffold* task in the VS Code Dapr extension to add Dapr support in the `launch.json` and `task.json` files. This time, we will manually edit the files.

Creating .NET solutions

We have previously provisioned our first .NET project. To test the multi-project debug configuration, we'll add a *second* Dapr project to our environment – in a great feat of imagination, let's name it `sample.microservice.webapi2`:

```
PS C:\Repos\dapr-samples\chapter02\sample.microservice.webapi>
cd ..
PS C:\Repos\dapr-samples\chapter02> dotnet new webapi -o
sample.microservice.webapi
2
The template "ASP.NET Core Web API" was created successfully.

Processing post-creation actions...
Running 'dotnet restore' on sample.microservice.webapi2\sample.
microservice.webapi2.csproj...
   Restore completed in 152,92 ms for C:\Repos\dapr-samples\
chapter02\sample.microse
rvice.webapi2\sample.microservice.webapi2.csproj.

Restore succeeded.
```

For brevity, the newly created .NET project should receive the same changes we applied to our first sample in the previous chapter.

With two ASP.NET projects, we could use a solution file to combine them together – the .NET CLI does have the ability to create an empty `.sln` file and add projects to it:

```
PS C:\Repos\dapr-samples\chapter02> dotnet new sln
The template "Solution File" was created successfully.
```

```
PS C:\Repos\dapr-samples\chapter02> dotnet sln add c:\Repos\
dapr-samples\chapter02\sample.microservice.webapi\sample.
microservice.webapi.csproj
```

The solution file is ready; we can now prepare the debugging configuration.

Launching the configuration

As we intend to debug `sample.microservice.webapi` (our original project) and `sample.microservice.webapi2` at the same time, the two .NET projects and Dapr application need to be running at the same time.

It is required that each ASP.NET should be hosted on a different port, and each Dapr application should have a different name, a unique HTTP, gRPC, and metrics port, and refer to the ASP.NET port as the Dapr app port.

The following code is a portion of the `launch.json` file:

```json
"version": "0.2.0",
"configurations": [
{
    "name": ".NET Core Launch w/Dapr (webapi)",
    "type": "coreclr",
    "request": "launch",
    "preLaunchTask": "daprd-debug-webapi",
    "program": "${workspaceFolder}/sample.microservice.
    webapi/bin/Debug/netcoreapp3.1/sample.microservice.
    webapi.dll",
    "args": [],
    "cwd": "${workspaceFolder}/sample.microservice.
    webapi",
    "stopAtEntry": false,
    "env": {
        "ASPNETCORE_ENVIRONMENT": "Development",
        "ASPNETCORE_URLS": "http://+:5001"
    },
    "sourceFileMap": {
        "/Views": "${workspaceFolder}/Views"
    },
    "postDebugTask": "daprd-down-webapi"
},
{

    "name": ".NET Core Launch w/Dapr (webapi2)",
    "type": "coreclr",
    "request": "launch",
    "preLaunchTask": "daprd-debug-webapi2",
    "program": "${workspaceFolder}/sample.microservice.
    webapi2/bin/Debug/netcoreapp3.1/sample.microservice.
    webapi2.dll",
    "args": [],
    "cwd": "${workspaceFolder}/sample.microservice.
    webapi2",
    "stopAtEntry": false,
    "env": {
        "ASPNETCORE_ENVIRONMENT": "Development",
        "ASPNETCORE_URLS": "http://+:5002",
    },
    "sourceFileMap": {
        "/Views": "${workspaceFolder}/Views"
    },
```

```
            "postDebugTask": "daprd-down-webapi2"
        }
    ]
}
```

As you can see from the launch configurations, each one refers to a corresponding `preLaunchTask` and a `postDebugTask`.

Tasks

The following is an extract from the `tasks: [...]` in the `task.json` file. You can find the complete configuration file in the sample directory:

```
... omitted ...
    {
        "label": "build-webapi",
        "command": "dotnet",
        "type": "process",
        "args": [
            "build",
            "${workspaceFolder}/sample.microservice.webapi/
             sample.microservice.webapi.csproj",
            "/property:GenerateFullPaths=true",
            "/consoleloggerparameters:NoSummary"
        ],
        "problemMatcher": "$msCompile"
    },
    {
        "appId": "hello-world",
        "appPort": 5001,
        "httpPort": 5010,
        "grpcPort": 50010,
        "metricsPort": 9091,
        "label": "daprd-debug-webapi",
        "type": "daprd",
        "problemMatcher": {
            "pattern": [
                {
                    "regexp": ".",
                    "file": 1,
                    "location": 2,
                    "message": 3
                }
```

```
                    ],
                    "background": {
                        "beginsPattern": "^.*starting Dapr
                        Runtime.*",
                        "endsPattern": "^.*waiting on port.*"
                    }
                },
                "dependsOn": "build-webapi"
            },
            {

                "appId": "hello-world",
                "label": "daprd-down-webapi",
                "type": "daprd-down"
            }
... omitted ...
```

In the previous snippet, you can see that for the hello-world service, corresponding to the project sample.microservice.webapi, the configuration adopts a set of "appPort": 5001, "httpPort": 5010, and "grpcPort": 50010, "metricsPort": 9091.

By contrast, the salute-world service configuration adopts other non-conflicting ports for the settings appPort, httpPort, grpcPort, and metricsPort.

It is worth noting that in the configuration file, two sets of tasks for build, dapr-debug (which launches the Dapr app), and dapr-down (to stop and cleanup) have been created, one for each project.

I also had to edit the path to each project's folder with the pattern "${workspaceFolder}/<project path>/<file>" wherever a reference to the project's file or library is needed.

Launching debug sessions individually

With these configurations, we can individually launch the integrated .NET and Dapr debugging experience in VS Code for each project. In the following screenshot, you can see the two debug configurations being recognized in VS Code:

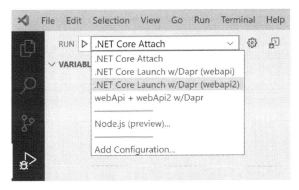

Figure 2.3 – Debug launch configurations in VS Code

We can test that each project is properly built, gets exposed (locally) as an ASP.NET endpoint, and then a Dapr CLI debugger is launched for each application.

As a simple test, in the following snippet, let's invoke the two Dapr applications via `curl`, while these are in debugging mode in VS Code:

```
PS C:\> curl http://localhost:5010/v1.0/invoke/hello-world/
method/hello
Hello, World
PS C:\> curl http://localhost:5020/v1.0/invoke/salute-world/
method/salute
I salute you, my dear World.
```

Our first two sample Dapr services can be invoked via the Dapr runtime. Let's try to launch a debug session next.

Launching compound debug sessions

We are not done yet: the last objective is to instruct VS Code to build and launch the two Dapr applications at the same time, instead of having the user individually launch the configuration for each project. This can be achieved with a compound task in VS Code. See `https://code.visualstudio.com/docs/editor/debugging#_compound-launch-configurations` for more information.

A compound launch configuration starts multiple debug sessions in parallel. All we need to do is refer to the previously defined configurations in `launch.json`:

```
"compounds":
    [
        {
            "name": "webApi + webApi2 w/Dapr",
            "configurations": [".NET Core Launch w/Dapr (webapi)",
```

```
      ".NET Core Launch w/Dapr (webapi2)"]
  }
]
```

As we can see from the following screenshot, we have both of the VS Code debug sessions active and both Dapr applications we previously defined, **hello-world** and **salute-world**, are active:

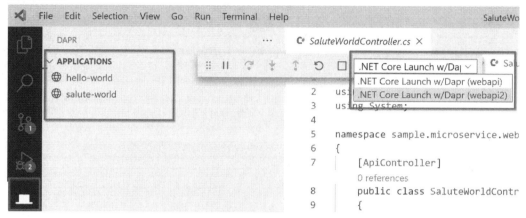

Figure 2.4 – Dapr debug session in VS Code

As the Dapr applications have been launched from the Dapr CLI debugger, they appear in the context of the Dapr extension for VS Code, as shown in *Figure 2.4*, but they do not arise from the Dapr CLI: the dapr list command or browsing the Dapr dashboard will show no applications running.

This completes our mission: we are now able to quickly enter a debug session that encompasses all the projects for microservices and other libraries we need.

Using Tye with Dapr

I find the multi-target debugging provided by VS Code a rewarding experience for Dapr solutions with several projects; nevertheless, there are always many options to accomplish the same task. One option for this particular task is **Tye**.

A new open source initiative by .NET Foundation, Project Tye is currently under development as an experimental project. For more information, check out the documentation at https://github.com/dotnet/tye/blob/master/docs/.

Project Tye is a tool to make developing, testing, and deploying microservices and distributed applications easier. Let's explore Project Tye in conjunction with Dapr!

Installing Tye

As an evolving project, refer to the Tye documentation for the latest information. You can use the most recent public version or a daily build:

```
PS C:\Windows\System32> dotnet tool install -g Microsoft.Tye
--version "0.5.0-alpha.20555.1"
You can invoke the tool using the following command: tye
Tool 'microsoft.tye' (version '0.5.0-alpha.20555.1') was
successfully installed.
```

It is that simple! Tye is now ready to be configured in our .NET solution.

Using Tye

In the root folder of the project structure, we initialize the .yaml file to instruct Tye on how to deal with the ASP.NET projects and Dapr configurations:

```
PS C:\Repos\dapr-samples\chapter02> tye init
Created 'C:\Repos\dapr-samples\chapter02\tye.yaml'.
Time Elapsed: 00:00:00:34
```

The preceding command creates a tye.yaml with the following content:

```
name: hello-world-debug
services:
- name: dapr-microservice-webapi
  project: sample.microservice.webapi/sample.microservice.
  webapi.csproj
- name: dapr-microservice-webapi2
  project: sample.microservice.webapi2/sample.microservice.
  webapi2.csproj
```

As I already had a solution file, Tye recognized the presence of the two projects. In our previous samples, we used the different Dapr app-ids, hello-world and salute-world; we will fix this in the next step.

By mutuating the Dapr recipe from the Tye repository at https://github.com/dotnet/tye/blob/master/samples/dapr/tye.yaml, I changed the default configuration to the following:

```
name: hello-world-debug
extensions:
- name: dapr
```

The only change has been adding `extensions` with `name: dapr`.

A caveat: as I have already initialized Dapr on my local environment, Redis is already in place. Therefore I left it out of the Tye configuration by commenting it.

From a command line (Windows Terminal or VS Code terminal window), we can launch Tye with the `tye run` command:

```
PS C:\Repos\dapr-samples\chapter02> tye run
```

From the following output, we can see how Tye launches our Dapr applications:

```
Loading Application Details...
Launching Tye Host...

[21:23:05 INF] Executing application from C:\Repos\dapr-
samples\chapter02\tye.yaml
[21:23:05 INF] Dashboard running on http://127.0.0.1:8000
[21:23:06 INF] Building projects
[21:23:07 INF] Launching service hello-world-dapr_dc1ac8cb-5:
daprd -app-id hello-world -app-port 60146 -dapr-grpc-port 60150
--dapr-http-port 60151 --metrics-port 60152 --placement-address
localhost:50005 -log-level debug
[21:23:07 INF] Launching service hello-world_613eee7d-f: C:\
Repos\dapr-samples\chapter02\sample.microservice.webapi\bin\
Debug\netcoreapp3.1\sample.microservice.webapi.exe
[21:23:07 INF] Launching service salute-world-dapr_90068b8d-4:
daprd -app-id salute-world -app-port 60148 -dapr-grpc-port
60153 --dapr-http-port 60154 --metrics-port 60155 --placement-
address localhost:50005 -log-level debug
[21:23:07 INF] Launching service salute-world_2f0e4504-2: C:\
Repos\dapr-samples\chapter02\sample.microservice.webapi2\bin\
Debug\netcoreapp3.1\sample.microservice.webapi2.exe
[21:23:07 INF] hello-world-dapr_dc1ac8cb-5 running on
process id 19140 bound to https://localhost:60150, http://
localhost:60151, http://localhost:60152
[21:23:07 INF] Replica hello-world-dapr_dc1ac8cb-5 is moving to
a ready state
[21:23:07 INF] hello-world_613eee7d-f running on process id
21224 bound to http://localhost:60146, https://localhost:60147
[21:23:07 INF] salute-world-dapr_90068b8d-4 running on
process id 16748 bound to https://localhost:60153, http://
localhost:60154, http://localhost:60155
[21:23:07 INF] Replica hello-world_613eee7d-f is moving to a
ready state
```

```
[21:23:07 INF] salute-world_2f0e4504-2 running on process id
23832 bound to http://localhost:60148, https://localhost:60149
[21:23:07 INF] Replica salute-world-dapr_90068b8d-4 is moving
to a ready state
[21:23:07 INF] Replica salute-world_2f0e4504-2 is moving to a
ready state
[21:23:08 INF] Selected process 23832.
[21:23:08 INF] Selected process 21224.
[21:23:08 INF] Listening for event pipe events for salute-
world_2f0e4504-2 on process id 23832
[21:23:08 INF] Listening for event pipe events for hello-
world_613eee7d-f on process id 21224
```

From the command output, we can observe that Tye launches the Dapr CLI debugger (daprd), referring to the corresponding Dapr application for the ASP.NET project, all by providing dynamic ports.

The Tye tool offers a portal from which you can access useful .NET metrics about the running processes:

Name	Type	Source	Bindings	Replicas	Restarts	Logs
hello-world	Project	C:\Repos\dapr-samples\chapter02\hello-world-debug\dapr.microservice. webapi\dapr.microservice.webapi.csproj	http://localhost:60146 https://localhost:60147	1/1	0	View
salute-world	Project	C:\Repos\dapr-samples\chapter02\hello-world-debug\dapr.microservice. webapi2\dapr.microservice.webapi2.csproj	http://localhost:60148 https://localhost:60149	1/1	0	View
hello-world-dapr	Executable		https://localhost:60150 http://localhost:60151 http://localhost:60152	1/1	0	View
salute-world-dapr	Executable		https://localhost:60153 http://localhost:60154 http://localhost:60155	1/1	0	View

Figure 2.5 – Tye portal

In *Figure 2.5*, you can see the Tye portal showing our Dapr services and the corresponding Dapr sidecars.

The --debug * option of the Tye command waits for VS Code debug sessions to be attached to each service: from Tye portal logs, you will see the message Waiting for debugger to attach....

In VS Code, we can leverage the *.NET Core attach* debug configuration, selecting the corresponding ASP.NET process, as we did at the beginning of this chapter, for each of our sample projects.

You might consider the option to customize the VS Code *.NET Core attach* to provide support for multiple projects, similar to what we did previously with the *.NET Core Launch w/Dapr (webapi)* debug configuration.

Once the VS Code debug session has started, we can invoke our Dapr applications:

```
PS C:\> curl http://localhost:60151/v1.0/invoke/hello-world/
method/hello
Hello, World
```

The first Dapr service responded, next we test the second one:

```
PS C:\> curl http://localhost:60154/v1.0/invoke/salute-world/
method/salute
I salute you, my dear World.
```

The Tye tool is useful in the contexts of both debugging .NET solutions and deploying them. Its integration with Dapr greatly simplifies the debugging experience.

With Tye, we have completed the discussion on Dapr's debugging options.

Summary

In this chapter, you have learned how to take advantage of several available options to debug C# Dapr projects, leveraging VS Code debug capabilities and configurations, the Dapr CLI itself, and Project Tye.

Getting comfortable with Tye and the Dapr CLI is also important as these will be the most frequently used approaches to launch our Dapr application in the testing phase.

In the next chapter, we will explore in more depth how services are invoked within Dapr.

Section 2: Building Microservices with Dapr

With newly acquired knowledge about the Dapr basics, you'll learn why microservices architecture is important and how Dapr can help you on this journey.

This section has the following chapters:

- *Chapter 3, Service-to-Service Invocation*
- *Chapter 4, Introducing State Management*
- *Chapter 5, Publish and Subscribe*
- *Chapter 6, Resource Bindings*
- *Chapter 7, Using Actors*

3
Service-to-Service Invocation

This chapter will instruct you on how services can discover and invoke each other via the **Distributed Application Runtime** (**Dapr**) infrastructure.

In this chapter, we are going to cover the following main topics:

- How services work in Dapr
- Service invocation with the .NET SDK
- HTTP and gRPC for Dapr services

With hands-on examples, we will understand how to implement services and invoke them from other applications, which can be either aware of Dapr as they rely on its SDK or unaware of the presence of Dapr as they just invoke a local HTTP endpoint.

Before we start using service-to-service invocation, a building block of Dapr, using an example, let's understand how it works.

Technical requirements

The code for this sample can be found on GitHub at `https://github.com/PacktPublishing/Practical-Microservices-with-Dapr-and-.NET/tree/main/chapter03`.

In this chapter, the working area for scripts and code is expected to be `<repository path>\chapter03\`. In my local environment, it is `C:\Repos\dapr-samples\chapter03`.

Please refer to the *Setting up Dapr* section in *Chapter 1, Introducing Dapr*, for a complete guide on the tools needed to develop with Dapr and work with the samples.

How services work in Dapr

In this section, we will learn how Dapr provides our microservices with the ability to interact directly via service-to-service invocation.

Services are the centerpiece of Dapr. A Dapr service enables the developer to easily make the API of a microservice discoverable and reachable to other components inside the hosting environment, whether it be a self-hosted or a Kubernetes cluster.

In this section, we will understand how a service can send and retrieve information to and from another service, using a practical example derived from our initial project.

The Dapr service invocation API, which we will leverage via the abstraction offered by the Dapr .NET SDK, provides discovery, retry logic, and reliable communication with standard protocols such as HTTP and gRPC.

In previous chapters, we built a few Dapr service samples, but we must give proper attention to the details, which we will do in this chapter. How can a service be reached via Dapr? This is going to be the focus of this chapter:

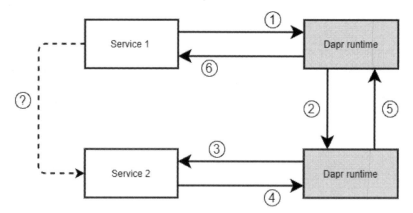

Figure 3.1 – Service-to-service invocation in Dapr

In *Figure 3.1*, we can visualize the path requests and responses taken to reach a specific service, traversing the Dapr runtime, which is running in a sidecar. In our local development environment, this is a simple interaction between local processes, while on Kubernetes, it will be a sidecar container automatically injected by Dapr into each of our application's pods.

This is what happens during service-to-service invocation, as shown in *Figure 3.1*:

1. Once **Service 1** makes a call intended to reach **Service 2**, the call from **Service 1** reaches the Dapr runtime on the local sidecar, which discovers the location for **Service 2**.

2. The runtime on the local sidecar forwards the request to the Dapr local sidecar of **Service 2**.

3. This Dapr sidecar invokes **Service 2** on the configured application port.

4. The same sidecar receives back the result from the application logic.

5. The result is in turn returned by **Service 2** Dapr's sidecar to **Service 1** Dapr's sidecar.

6. At last, the result of the request to **Service 2** is returned to **Service 1**.

We will now introduce a new project that will help us navigate the more complex patterns of Dapr.

Introducing our sample architecture

In order to navigate the concepts of Dapr throughout this book, we could use the help of a common theme to guide us: I thought that a fictional scenario, with an architecture that we will implement together, might be a good approach for the samples.

Therefore, let's introduce the architecture of *Biscotti Brutti ma Buoni*: in order to explore Dapr, it's time to move away from the "Hello world" kind of samples and shift to a hypothetical e-commerce scenario, which will be presented from different perspectives to illustrate each of Dapr's capabilities over the course of the following chapters.

The architecture of the fictional e-commerce site *Biscotti Brutti ma Buoni* (which means *ugly but good cookies* in Italian) is further discussed from a microservices perspective in *Appendix, Microservices Architectures with Dapr*.

In a nutshell, the *Biscotti Brutti ma Buoni* website sells cookies to consumers, offering the ability to customize them. Cookies are manufactured all day and, therefore, keeping track of their availability is important. Hopefully, this scenario will help us learn new topics from a practical standpoint and will make it easier to understand and implement them.

Now that we have shared a common context, we can learn how to implement Dapr services in ASP.NET.

Introducing service-to-service invocation

As the first sample in our fictional scenario, let's consider an ordering system whose API receives a fully composed order with items and quantities. Its first objective is to allocate the requested items, by reserving the quantities if it is a new order, or adjusting the quantities if the order has been updated after the initial submission. We can depict two microservices: **Order** and **Reservation**:

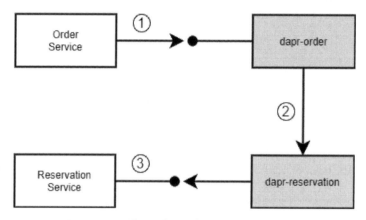

Figure 3.2 – The Order and Reservation services

From clients outside of this partial perspective, the Order service receives a new or updated order. It needs to interact with Reservation, another Dapr service:

1. From the Order service, which is an ASP.NET web API, a number of calls to the Dapr local endpoint are made in the following form:

    ```
    POST http://localhost:3500/v1.0/invoke/reservation/
    method/reserveitem
    ```

    The methods supported by the Dapr service are POST, GET, DELETE, and PUT. In this example, we could choose to react to POST for new orders and PUT for updated orders. The default Dapr sidecar port is 3500 inside the pod of a Kubernetes environment, while in our local development, each sidecar has to use a different port number, and reservation is the name of the Dapr service we want to reach to invoke the reserveitem method.

    The communication between the service and the local sidecar can happen over HTTP or gRPC.

2. The local Dapr sidecar identifies the Dapr sidecar capable of reaching the Reservation service and forwards the request.

   This leg of communication between Dapr sidecars, outside of the developer's control, happens via gRPC and is secured via mutual TLS.

   In a Kubernetes hosting environment, chances are it will traverse different nodes over the network.

3. The Dapr sidecar for the Reservation service has the knowledge to reach the service on the local port to request the `reserveitem` route. As an ASP.NET API, it is likely to be exposed on port `80` via Kestrel as a container in a Kubernetes pod, while in local development, we have to use different ports to avoid conflicts. The call would have this form:

```
POST http://localhost:80/reserveitem
```

   The Reservation service can be exposed as HTTP or gRPC.

After covering the basics of how a service can be reached via Dapr compared to directly via the ASP.NET endpoint, let's find out how name resolution works.

Name resolution

Dapr relies on the Kubernetes name resolution in this hosting mode, and on mDNS while in self-hosted mode, such as in a local development environment.

Service discovery is the component that enables any request to a Dapr sidecar (process or container) to identify the corresponding sidecar and to reach the intended service endpoint.

We now have our set of microservices to put to good use: the next sections will be dedicated to .NET, as well as HTTP and gRPC service invocation methods.

Service invocation with the .NET SDK

The best approach to understand how the Dapr .NET Core SDK supports service-to-service invocation is to thoroughly examine a sample project.

These are the steps that we will follow:

1. Create a project for the Order service.

2. Configure Dapr in ASP.NET.

3. Implement Dapr with an ASP.NET controller.

4. Create a project for the Reservation service.

5. Prepare debugging configuration.

6. Implement Dapr with ASP.NET routing.

We will start by creating a project for the first Dapr application in our solution.

Creating a project for the Order service

When creating the project for a Dapr service, we start from the `webapi` template:

```
PS C:\Repos\dapr-samples> cd .\chapter03\
PS C:\Repos\dapr-samples\chapter03> dotnet new webapi -o
sample.microservice.order
The template "ASP.NET Core Web API" was created successfully.

Processing post-creation actions...
Running 'dotnet restore' on sample.microservice.order\sample.
microservice.order.csproj...
  Restore completed in 151,4 ms for C:\Repos\dapr-samples\
chapter03\sample.microservice.order\sample.microservice.order.
csproj.

Restore succeeded.
```

We have created our project from the template. Next, we will configure ASP.NET.

Configuring Dapr in ASP.NET

Dapr provides several libraries via NuGet (`https://www.nuget.org/profiles/dapr.io`) for .NET. The most relevant ones are as follows:

- `Dapr.AspNetCore`
- `Dapr.Client`

With the following command, we can add the packages to our .NET project:

```
PS C:\Repos\dapr-samples\chapter03\sample.microservice.order>
dotnet add package Dapr.AspNetCore --version 0.12.0-preview01
```

We now have an ASP.NET project with full support for Dapr. Let's add some Dapr-specific code to our ASP.NET controller.

Implementing Dapr with an ASP.NET controller

We can create an ASP.NET controller to support the Dapr application's method call:

```csharp
using System;
using System.Threading.Tasks;
using Dapr;
using Dapr.Client;
using Dapr.Client.Http;
using Microsoft.AspNetCore.Mvc;

namespace sample.microservice.order.Controllers
{
    [ApiController]
    public class OrderController : ControllerBase
    {
        [HttpPost("order")]
        public async Task<ActionResult<Guid>> SubmitOrder(Order
        order, [FromServices] DaprClient daprClient)
        {
            Console.WriteLine("Enter submit order");

            order.Id = Guid.NewGuid();

            HTTPExtension httpExtension = new HTTPExtension()
            {
                Verb = HTTPVerb.Post
            };
            foreach (var item in order.Items)
            {
                var data = new { product = item.ProductCode,
                 quantity = item.Quantity };
                await daprClient.InvokeMethodAsync<object>(
                "reservation-service", "reserve", data,
                httpExtension);
            }
            Console.WriteLine($"Submitted order {order.Id}");

            return order.Id;
        }
    }
}
```

n the `SubmitOrder` method signature, you will notice that the parameter with the `DaprClient` type has been injected via ASP.NET: the reason why we had to modify the sequence in `Startup.cs` is also to support the dependency injection of the Dapr components.

`daprClient` is used here to invoke another service, but it gives our code access to the rest of the Dapr components, such as publish/subscribe, state stores, and so on.

The rest of the code is very basic, with no significant logic and, especially, no state is stored anywhere. This part will be developed in *Chapter 4, Introducing State Management*.

Once the order method of the Dapr `order-service` application is invoked, it cycles through the received payload to invoke the other application.

In `InvokeMethodAsync<object>("reservation-service", "reserve", data, httpExtension)`, we can recognize the `"reservation-service"` application name, the `"reserve"` method, the payload, and `httpExtension`: as we are sending a `POST` request, we have to specify all of it; if it were `GET`, this would not have been necessary.

Our Dapr Order service is complete; we can now create the Reservation service.

Creating a project for the Reservation service

We can now add the project for the Order service to a solution and create a new project for the Reservation service.

We also add the same package reference to the Dapr SDK as we did in the previous project, and we are ready to configure the debugging configuration.

Preparing the debugging configuration

I followed the debugging instructions from *Chapter 2, Debugging Dapr Solutions*, to create a compound launch configuration in **Visual Studio Code (VS Code)** for the projects corresponding to the two Dapr applications. In the samples, you will find `launch.json` and `tasks.json` properly configured.

I also included the `tye.yaml` configuration. Please note that in this sample, we will directly launch the applications via the Dapr CLI

Next, we will develop the second ASP.NET Dapr service.

Implementing Dapr with ASP.NET routing

In ASP.NET, you can control the routing of requests to controllers via attributes and conventional routing. Alternatively, you could also specify your application methods by mapping the routes directly to a method.

By following the approach from the Dapr document in the ASP.NET Core routing sample at `https://github.com/dapr/dotnet-sdk/tree/master/samples/AspNetCore/RoutingSample`, this is what our initial draft for a Reservation service could look like:

```
using System;
using System.Text.Json;
using System.Threading.Tasks;
using Dapr.Client;
using Microsoft.AspNetCore.Builder;
using Microsoft.AspNetCore.Hosting;
using Microsoft.AspNetCore.Http;
using Microsoft.Extensions.Configuration;
using Microsoft.Extensions.DependencyInjection;
using Microsoft.Extensions.Hosting;


namespace sample.microservice.reservation
{
    public class Startup
    {
        public Startup(IConfiguration configuration)
        {
            Configuration = configuration;
        }

        public IConfiguration Configuration { get; }
        public void ConfigureServices(IServiceCollection
        services)
        {
            services.AddControllers().AddDapr(builder =>
                builder.UseJsonSerializationOptions(
                    new JsonSerializerOptions()
                    {
                        PropertyNamingPolicy =
                        JsonNamingPolicy.CamelCase,
                        PropertyNameCaseInsensitive = true,
                    }));
        }
```

```
public void Configure(IApplicationBuilder
app, IWebHostEnvironment env, JsonSerializerOptions
serializerOptions)
{
    if (env.IsDevelopment())
    {
        app.UseDeveloperExceptionPage();
    }
    app.UseRouting();
    app.UseAuthorization();
    app.UseEndpoints(endpoints =>
    {
        endpoints.MapPost("reserve", Reserve);
    });
... omitted ...
```

The previous section of Startup.cs deals with the ASP.NET configuration and startup, which configure the reserve route to the Reserve method in the same class and file, as you can see in the following snippet:

```
... omitted ...
    async Task Reserve(HttpContext context)
    {
        Console.WriteLine("Enter Reservation");

        var client = context.RequestServices.
        GetRequiredService<DaprClient>();

        ... omitted ...
        context.Response.ContentType = "application/
        json";
        await JsonSerializer.SerializeAsync(context.
        Response.Body, storedItem, serializerOptions);
    }
}
}
}
```

We are now ready to start the testing and debug of our newly created project: will it work?

Instead of launching the two applications via VS Code, this time we will start the applications with the Dapr CLI from separate terminal windows with these commands, each to be executed in their respective project folders. We first run the "order-service" application:

```
dapr run --app-id "order-service" --app-port "5001" --dapr-
grpc-port "50010" --dapr-http-port "5010" -- dotnet run
--urls="http://+:5001"
```

We then run the "reservation-service" application:

```
dapr run --app-id "reservation-service" --app-port "5002"
--dapr-grpc-port "50020" --dapr-http-port "5020" -- dotnet run
--urls="http://+:5002"
```

While working in self-hosted mode, as in our development environment, we have to carefully avoid port conflicts.

The output of the Dapr CLI can be verbose, though interesting, so for the sake of brevity, these are the lines that tell us that the Order service launch has been successful and it is ready to be invoked:

```
PS C:\Repos\dapr-samples\chapter03\sample.microservice.order>
dapr run --app-id "order-service" --app-port "5001" --dapr-
grpc-port "50010" --dapr-http-port "5010" -- dotnet run
--urls="http://+:5001"
Starting Dapr with id order-service. HTTP Port: 5010. gRPC
Port: 50010

… omitted …

Updating metadata for app command: dotnet run
--urls=http://+:5001
You're up and running! Both Dapr and your app logs will appear
here.
```

Another confirmation that both applications are up and running comes from the `dapr list` output:

```
PS C:\Windows\System32> dapr list
  APP ID                 HTTP PORT  GRPC PORT  APP PORT   COMMAND
AGE  CREATED               PID
  order-service          5010         50010      5001       dotnet
run --urls...  4m   2020-09-12 15:31.56  14280
  reservation-service  5020           50020      5002       dotnet
run --urls...  4m   2020-09-12 15:32.09  25552
```

I can now post a JSON payload to the `http://localhost:5010/v1.0/invoke/order-service/method/order` Dapr URL and see the result, and then verify the traces in each of our application's terminal windows.

When I'm dealing with a JSON payload, I prefer to use Postman or the VS Code REST Client extension (`https://marketplace.visualstudio.com/items?itemName=humao.rest-client`), which offers a better experience, even if we are not using VS Code for debugging:

```
POST http://localhost:5010/v1.0/invoke/order-service/method/
order HTTP/1.1
content-type: application/json

{
  "Items": [
    {
      "ProductCode": "cookie1",
      "Quantity": 3
    },
    {
      "ProductCode": "ultimate-cookie5",
      "Quantity": 2
    }
  ]
}
```

We receive back a new order ID from the `order-service` Dapr application:

```
HTTP/1.1
200 OK
Connection: close
Date: Tue, 13 Oct 2020 17:54:20 GMT
Content-Type: application/json;
charset=utf-8
```

```
Server: Kestrel
Transfer-Encoding: chunked

"15586359-7413-4838-afde-9adb57ce2d4b"
```

The following output is from the `order-service` application:

```
== APP == Enter submit order

== APP == Submitted order 15586359-7413-4838-afde-9adb57ce2d4b
```

Yes, that is our newly submitted order ID!

This is the `reservation-service` output:

```
== APP == Enter Reservation

== APP == Reservation of cookie1 is now -3

== APP == Enter Reservation

== APP == Reservation of ultimate-cookie5 is now -2
```

For each of the items in the submitted order, `order-service` invokes a `reservation-service` method.

Recap

At this stage, any change is ephemeral as no state is preserved. Nevertheless, we successfully built two Dapr services with ASP.NET, using the controller and basic routing approaches, and using `DaprClient` made available via dependency injection, we established a communication channel via Dapr between the two microservices.

The next section is dedicated to HTTP and gRPC service invocation, which will make things considerably more interesting and complex.

HTTP and gRPC for Dapr services

gRPC is a *high-performance, open source, universal RPC framework* that became extremely popular in the inter-microservices communication space because of its efficiency. gRPC is based on HTTP/2 for transport and adopts the binary serialization format Protobuf.

> **Note**
>
> There are several documents and blog posts on how to implement gRPC servers in Dapr, including articles from the .NET documentation on gRPC, `https://docs.microsoft.com/en-us/aspnet/core/tutorials/grpc/grpc-start?view=aspnetcore-3.1&tabs=visual-studio-code`, and the (not specific to .NET) Dapr documentation on the gRPC service, `https://docs.dapr.io/operations/configuration/grpc/`.

gRPC is a Cloud Native Computing Foundation incubated project.

gRPC in ASP.NET Core

In ASP.NET Core, we are so used to the combination of HTTP and JSON that we tend to think of these two as the only transport and format choices for a web API.

With the growth in popularity of gRPC and the ability to use it from ASP.NET Core too, we can see it as an alternative for a web API: gRPC requires HTTP/2 with payload serialized in Protobuf format; for more information, I suggest you read this introduction: `https://grpc.io/docs/what-is-grpc/introduction/`.

In the context of .NET, this document, `https://docs.microsoft.com/en-us/aspnet/core/grpc/comparison?view=aspnetcore-3.1`, explains the different perspectives.

The autonomy of a microservice

Considering the sample we have built so far in this chapter, we will try to expose the Reservation service with gRPC and also instruct the Dapr sidecar of the `reservation-service` application to communicate over gRPC on the last leg of the communication. These are the steps:

1. Create a new Reservation service to be exposed via gRPC.

2. Copy the Dapr server proto to the project.

3. Implement the necessary service scope.

4. Configure the project for gRPC with Dapr.

5. Register `reservation-service` as a Dapr application via gRPC.

6. Test the Order service with the evolved Reservation service.

If we succeed in changing the implementation of a service and the way Dapr interacts with it, we would also demonstrate how Dapr makes it easy to build microservices that are autonomous, as they can have an independent evolution without impacting any other microservice.

Creating reservation-service

As a starting point, create a new .NET project with a gRPC template with the following command-line command:

```
dotnet new grpc -o sample.microservice.reservation-grpc
```

The project is now ready in the working area of our sample.

Copying the Dapr proto

The current version of the Dapr `.proto` files, which contain the contract definition of the Dapr API, are located at `https://github.com/dapr/dapr/tree/master/dapr/proto`.

We install the .NET `dotnet-grpc` tool to help us in adding a project reference to the Dapr `common.proto` and `appcallback.proto` files and to copy the files to a folder inside the project, keeping the same structure:

```
dotnet tool install -g dotnet-grpc
```

```
dotnet-grpc add-url -o "Protos/dapr/proto/runtime/v1/
appcallback.proto" -i Protos/ -s Server https://raw.
githubusercontent.com/dapr/dapr/master/dapr/proto/runtime/v1/
appcallback.proto
```

```
dotnet-grpc add-url -o "Protos/dapr/proto/common/v1/common.
proto" -i Protos/ -s Server https://raw.githubusercontent.com/
dapr/dapr/master/dapr/proto/common/v1/common.proto
```

These commands leveraging the `dotnet-grpc` tool will update the `.csproj` file with the `Protobuf` references:

```
<ItemGroup>
    <Protobuf Include="Protos/dapr/proto/common/v1/common.
proto" GrpcServices="Server" AdditionalImportDirs="Protos/">
        <SourceUrl>https://raw.githubusercontent.com/dapr/dapr/
master/dapr/proto/common/v1/common.proto</SourceUrl>
    </Protobuf>
    <Protobuf Include="Protos/dapr/proto/runtime/
v1/appcallback.proto" GrpcServices="Server"
AdditionalImportDirs="Protos/">
        <SourceUrl>https://raw.githubusercontent.com/dapr/dapr/
master/dapr/proto/runtime/v1/appcallback.proto</SourceUrl>
    </Protobuf>
  </ItemGroup>
```

As soon as the `.proto` files are referenced, the classes mapping the proto definitions will be generated automatically in the background.

Service implementation

A gRPC service has some differences in the `Startup.cs` file:

```
using Microsoft.AspNetCore.Builder;
using Microsoft.AspNetCore.Hosting;
using Microsoft.AspNetCore.Http;
using Microsoft.Extensions.DependencyInjection;
using Microsoft.Extensions.Hosting;

namespace sample.microservice.reservation_grpc
{
    public class Startup
    {
        public void ConfigureServices(IServiceCollection
        services)
        {
            services.AddGrpc(options =>
            {
                options.EnableDetailedErrors = true;
            });

            services.AddRouting();
        }
```

```
        public void Configure(IApplicationBuilder app,
        IWebHostEnvironment env)
        {
            if (env.IsDevelopment())
            {
                app.UseDeveloperExceptionPage();
            }

            app.UseRouting();
            app.UseEndpoints(endpoints =>
            {
                endpoints.MapGrpcService<ReservationService>();

                endpoints.MapGet("/", async context =>
                {
                    await context.Response.
                    WriteAsync("Communication with gRPC
                    endpoints must be made through a gRPC
                    client. To learn how to create a client,
                    visit: https://go.microsoft.com/
                    fwlink/?linkid=2086909");
                });
            });
        }
    }
}
```

The way ASP.NET supports gRPC is similar to the routing approach.

The following is the gRPC implementation specific to a Dapr service:

```
using System;
using System.Threading.Tasks;
using Dapr.Client.Autogen.Grpc.v1;
using Dapr.AppCallback.Autogen.Grpc.v1;
using Google.Protobuf.WellKnownTypes;
using Grpc.Core;

namespace sample.microservice.reservation_grpc
{
    public class ReservationService : Dapr.AppCallback.Autogen.
    Grpc.v1.AppCallback.AppCallbackBase
    {
        public override Task<InvokeResponse>
        OnInvoke(InvokeRequest request, ServerCallContext
```

```
context)
{
    Console.WriteLine(request.Method);

    switch (request.Method)
    {
        case "reserve":
            var input = Extensions.
            FromAnyAsync<Item>(request.Data);

            var output = new Item{SKU=input.SKU,
            Quantity = - input.Quantity};

            return Task.FromResult(new InvokeResponse
            {Data = Extensions. ToAnyAsync<Item>(output)});
        default:
            Console.WriteLine("Method not supported");
            return Task.FromResult(new
            InvokeResponse());
    }
}

public override Task<ListInputBindingsResponse>
ListInputBindings(Empty request, ServerCallContext
context)
{
    return Task.FromResult(new
    ListInputBindingsResponse());
}

public override Task<ListTopicSubscriptionsResponse>
ListTopicSubscriptions(Empty request, ServerCallContext
context)
{
    return Task.FromResult(new
    ListTopicSubscriptionsResponse());
}
    }
}
```

The ReservationService class inherits the automatically generated Dapr.
AppCallback.Autogen.Grpc.v1.AppCallback.AppCallbackBase and it
implements the necessary methods.

Our embarrassingly simple code (for which you should leverage a mediator) implements the `OnInvoke(InvokeRequest request, ServerCallContext context)` method and returns an `InvokeResponse` type.

Test integration

In order to launch our service as a Dapr application, we have to change the way we use the Dapr CLI:

```
PS C:\Repos\dapr-samples\chapter03\sample.microservice.
reservation-grpc> dapr run --app-id "reservation-service"
--app-port "3000" --app-protocol grpc --dapr-grpc-port "50020"
-- dotnet run --urls="http://+:3000"

Starting Dapr with id reservation-service. HTTP Port: 55614.
gRPC Port: 50020
... omitted ...

== APP ==        Request starting HTTP/2 POST
http://127.0.0.1:3000/dapr.proto.runtime.v1.AppCallback/
ListInputBindings application/grpc

== APP ==        Executing endpoint 'gRPC - /dapr.proto.runtime.
v1.AppCallback/ListInputBindings'

== APP ==        Executed endpoint 'gRPC - /dapr.proto.runtime.
v1.AppCallback/ListInputBindings'

...

== APP ==        Request starting HTTP/2 POST
http://127.0.0.1:3000/dapr.proto.runtime.v1.AppCallback/
ListTopicSubscriptions application/grpc

... omitted ...

== APP ==        Executing endpoint 'gRPC - /dapr.proto.runtime.
v1.AppCallback/ListTopicSubscriptions'

== APP ==        Executed endpoint 'gRPC - /dapr.proto.runtime.
v1.AppCallback/ListTopicSubscriptions'

You're up and running! Both Dapr and your app logs will appear
here.
```

In the `dapr run --app-id "reservation-service" --app-port "3000"` `--app-protocol grpc --dapr-grpc-port "50020" -- dotnet run` `--urls="http://+:3000"` command, we specified that Dapr will interact with our service via gRPC.

We can launch the Order service untouched and unaware that the Reservation service shifted from the web API to gRPC:

```
dapr run --app-id "order-service" --app-port "5001" --dapr-
grpc-port "50010" --dapr-http-port "5010" -- dotnet run
--urls="http://+:5001"
```

As `order-service` already leveraged `DaprClient` from the Dapr .NET SDK, it will reach the evolved `reservation-service` using gRPC at each step.

Winning latency with gRPC

In this scenario, we have to consider the potential impact of a minuscule latency gain, obtained with service-to-service communication fully done with gRPC:

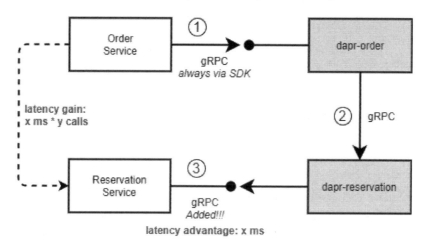

Figure 3.3 – Service-to-service invocation via gRPC

Figure 3.3 depicts how each small advantage can accrue significant latency reductions at large numbers of requests.

It's not this chapter's objective to discuss the pros and cons of gRPC, nor to convince you to favor exposing microservices to Dapr as gRPC services. In my perspective, in most cases, the advantages in productivity that come with the ASP.NET web API approach overcome the marginal latency gains with gRPC in the last leg, considering that Dapr already grants the benefit of gRPC inter-node latency.

We will dig deeper into the microservices paradigm by addressing the elephant in the room, that is, managing state within Dapr, in the next chapter.

Summary

This intense chapter introduced you to the most relevant building block of Dapr: service-to-service invocation.

We learned how to configure an ASP.NET project, how to decorate methods in a controller with Dapr's specific parameters, and how to interact from one Dapr service to another.

Finally, we discussed the more complex mechanics of a gRPC service in the context of Dapr.

You may have noticed that our sample microservices are not persisting their state yet: in the next chapter, we will explore how to use Dapr's state management building block.

4
Introducing State Management

State management for services and actors is a centerpiece of Dapr: this chapter will illustrate how a Dapr solution can manage the services' state with different store types.

These are the main topics that we will explore:

- Managing state in Dapr
- Stateful services in an e-commerce ordering system
- Azure Cosmos DB as a state store

Most, if not all, of our services and actors in the Dapr applications we are building have data persisted as state.

State could be the status of a request, kept aside to be able to return additional information about a complex interaction at a later stage, or it could be the central information managed by the service, such as the quantity of available product.

State management is equally important for a new, cloud-native solution built with Dapr and for an existing solution to which we are adding Dapr services.

We will learn how to configure and use state with Dapr. An overview of state management concepts is our starting point.

Technical requirements

The code for this sample can be found on GitHub at `https://github.com/ PacktPublishing/Practical-Microservices-with-Dapr-and-.NET/ tree/main/chapter04`.

In this chapter, the working area for scripts and code is expected to be `<repository path>\chapter04\`. In my local environment, it is `C:\Repos\dapr-samples\ chapter04`.

Please refer to the section entitled *Setting up Dapr* in *Chapter 1, Introducing Dapr*, for a complete guide on the tools needed to develop with Dapr and work with the samples.

Managing state in Dapr

In a microservice architecture, **state** is intended as the collection of information that defines the context in which the microservice operates. In this section, we will learn how state can be managed and how Dapr does it.

State, stateless, and stateful

The way state is managed defines whether a microservice is **stateful** (when it takes the responsibility of persisting state upon itself) or **stateless** (when the state is not in its scope of responsibility).

An example of a stateful microservice would be a shopping cart microservice that keeps the list of items in a central location (such as a database) so the customer can transparently migrate between different devices to continue their shopping experience. The shopping cart microservice could be designed by keeping the state in the host/node memory and enforcing a policy at the load balancer level to route all further interactions from the client to the original node.

Would it be a good idea, in the age of the cloud, to adopt this approach? It is not. To gain a higher level of resiliency in a modern architecture, the nodes should be considered as expendable resources that can fail without impacting the solution.

A good example of a stateless microservice is a machine learning model exposed via API, which, given a set of input parameters, would return a prediction. A microservice supporting a business activity is likely to count on a state. As the microservice should be able to scale to additional instances or restore from process or host failures, it does become increasingly relevant to keep the state externally, for example on a **Database as a Service (DBaaS)** offering, relieving our architecture of these hard to solve problems. The shopping cart microservice could also adopt a stateless approach by persisting the state on an external store.

With the reliable state API provided by Dapr, every microservice built with the Dapr runtime can be considered as a stateless service as it keeps its state in an external, configurable store. Next, we will see the many state stores currently supported in Dapr.

State stores in Dapr

A state store is a Dapr component that implements the reliable store interfaces.

At this stage in time of the Dapr project, several state stores have been provided by the team or contributed by the community, including the following:

- Azure Cosmos DB
- Azure Table Storage
- Azure SQL Server
- Couchbase
- AWS DynamoDB
- Memcached
- MongoDB
- Redis
- Cassandra
- PostgreSQL

The open and extensible capabilities of Dapr allows any party to implement additional state stores. You can find the state components of the Dapr project at its repository: `https://github.com/dapr/components-contrib/tree/master/state`.

Multiple stores can be configured in the same hosting environment, enabling your application to retrieve, update, or delete the state as a key/value (JSON serializable) pair.

In your local development environment, the Redis state store is configured by default, pointing to a Redis container deployed during the `dapr init` setup.

Each state store, depending on the database or service capabilities, may provide additional features. Let's start with transaction support.

Transactions

A Dapr state store can coordinate the queries to the database, resulting from the application's interaction with the Dapr state management building block, under a transactional context by implementing the `TransactionalStore` interface.

As of today, only a subset of state stores in Dapr support transactions:

- Azure Cosmos DB
- SQL Server
- MongoDB
- Redis
- PostgreSQL

A specific scenario requiring transaction support involves the Actor model in Dapr. We will explore this in more depth in *Chapter 7, Using Actors*.

Concurrency

Dapr gives developers control over concurrency in state manipulation by returning and accepting **ETag**. ETag is a metadata used to identify the version of a resource, in this case, a key/value pair in Dapr state management.

If the application retrieving the state retains the attached ETag, it can later re-attach it to an update request to prevent overwriting a newer state, which might have changed in the interim: if the ETag sent back to Dapr does not match the original one, the operation is rejected due to the first-write-wins approach.

By using the Dapr C# SDK, the ETag is managed transparently for you while dealing with state management. If no ETag is provided in the state change request, a last-write-wins approach is applied.

If you foresee a scenario in which your service will experience concurrent service requests, with ETag, your application can make sure unintended state overwrites are avoided.

Consistency

Consistency in state change requests can also be controlled by the application. If eventual consistency is preferred (this is the default), the state change is considered successful by Dapr as soon as the underlying state store acknowledges the write operation; if strong consistency is required instead by the application, Dapr waits for the state store to complete the write operation on all of its replicas.

Not all state stores support both eventual and strong consistency modes: the Azure Cosmos DB is one of those that does. You can learn more about the performance impact of consistency in the documentation available at `https://docs.microsoft.com/en-us/azure/cosmos-db/consistency-levels`.

By controlling the consistency, your application code can specify, for each operation, the risks versus benefits in retrieving and persisting a state.

Interaction with state stores

An application can directly invoke the Dapr sidecar via HTTP call `http://localhost:<daprPort>/v1.0/state/<storename>/<key>`, or you can leverage the abstraction offered by the SDK.

The following diagram depicts the interaction between your application and the Dapr sidecar, which, influenced by the component's configuration, leverages a state store:

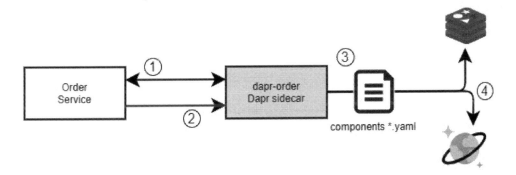

Figure 4.1 – State stores in Dapr

The diagram in *Figure 4.1* describes the steps of a state operation in Dapr. Let's explore these in detail:

1. The application invokes the local URL provided by the Dapr sidecar, for example, GET `http://localhost:<daprPort>/v1.0/state/shoppingcart/43`, to retrieve the state.

2. The Dapr state can be updated by an application with an HTTP POST request to the Dapr state API, `http://localhost:<daprPort>/v1.0/state/shoppingcart/43`. State can also be deleted with a DELETE request to the same Dapr endpoint.

3. The state stores available to the Dapr application are defined via `.yaml` files, present in a components folder, or applied to the Kubernetes configuration.

    To accommodate the request, a component named `shoppingcart` is expected to be configured.

4. While locally, Dapr could be using the Redis local container provided by Dapr, on Kubernetes, it could be relying on an external state such as Azure Cosmos DB. All we need is a change to the component's `.yaml` files.

The key of a Dapr state uses the same format on all state stores, by combining the application ID and the state key used in the application, with the format `<App ID>||<state key>`. Following the previous example, the key for the persisted record of the shopping cart on Redis or Cosmos DB would be `shoppingcart||43`.

Microservice architecture suggests keeping state, and data in general, separate. Nevertheless, with this approach, Dapr lets us use the same configured state store with different Dapr applications without the risk of key collisions. `43` in the context of `shoppingcart` will have a different composed key than the state record of `order` number `43`.

The following is a `yaml` file component that does use the local Redis container:

```yaml
apiVersion: dapr.io/v1alpha1
kind: Component
metadata:
  name: statestore
spec:
  type: state.redis
  metadata:
  - name: redisHost
```

```
      value: localhost:6379
  -   name: redisPassword
      value: ""
```

In the previous `yaml` file, a component of the `state.redis` type has been configured to connect to the Redis local instance.

The next section is dedicated to how a stateful service for a common e-commerce platform can be organized with Dapr.

Stateful services in an e-commerce ordering system

Moving forward with the Order-Reservation scenario introduced in the previous chapters, at this stage, we will focus on persisting the state in each Dapr application.

The following diagram anticipates the change in state management that we are going to apply to our microservices:

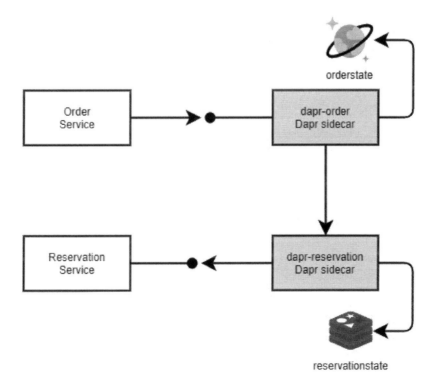

Figure 4.2 – Multiple state stores in Dapr

As you can see in *Figure 4.2*, the Dapr `reservation-service` service is going to use Redis as the state store, while `order-service` is going to leverage the Cosmos DB state store.

The following are the project structures used to support the Dapr applications `order-service` and `reservation-service`:

- `sample.microservice.dto.order`
- `sample.microservice.order`
- `sample.microservice.dto.reservation`
- `sample.microservice.reservation`

I decided to have separate **data transfer object (DTO)** libraries, which a service client can use to interact with the service itself, from the objects used to persist the state. This is just one of many possible approaches.

We start by implementing state management in `reservation-service`.

Stateful reservation-service

What makes the Dapr application's `reservation-service` a stateful service? The short answer is that the application keeps track of the balance quantity for items, evaluating the reservation request originating from the received orders.

`order-service` does not keep track of the item balance between one reservation and the next. Instead, it relies on `reservation-service` to manage this information and preserve it safely over time; this is what it is generally expected from a stateful service.

This is how we would like to interact with our ASP.NET service endpoint from a client:

```
POST http://localhost:5002/reserve HTTP/1.1
content-type: application/json

{
    "SKU": "cookie2",
    "Quantity": 2
}

###
GET http://localhost:5002/balance/cookie2 HTTP/1.1
```

From the preceding code, a /reserve method invoke accepts a reservation quantity and gives back the affected balance. The same information is returned if we invoke the /balance/<SKU> path. Next, we will learn how to manage the state with Dapr and .NET SDK.

Handling the Dapr state in ASP.NET controllers

The DaprClient class gives our code access to the Dapr runtime by abstracting the interaction with the API endpoint exposed by the sidecar.

An instance is made available to the Controller method via dependency injection. Thanks to .AddDapr, we need to add in ConfigureServices to Startup.cs:

```
public void ConfigureServices(IServiceCollection
services)
{
    services.AddControllers().AddDapr();

    services.AddSingleton(new JsonSerializerOptions()
    {
        PropertyNamingPolicy = JsonNamingPolicy.
        CamelCase,
        PropertyNameCaseInsensitive = true,
    });
}
```

In the following code snippets, you will see how daprClient gives access to states, services, and messages.

We can examine the following code in ReservationController.cs:

```
using System;
using System.Threading.Tasks;
using System.Collections.Generic;
using Dapr;
using Dapr.Client;
using Microsoft.AspNetCore.Mvc;
using sample.microservice.dto.reservation;
using sample.microservice.state.reservation;

namespace sample.microservice.reservation.Controllers
{
    [ApiController]
    public class OrderController : ControllerBase
    {
```

```
     public const string StoreName = "reservationstore";

     [HttpPost("reserve")]
     public async Task<ActionResult<Item>> Reserve(Item
     reservation, [FromServices] DaprClient daprClient)
     {
         Console.WriteLine("Enter item reservation");

         var state = await daprClient.
         GetStateEntryAsync<ItemState>(StoreName,
         reservation.SKU);
         state.Value ??= new ItemState() { SKU =
         reservation.SKU, Changes = new
         List<ItemReservation>() };

         // update balance
         state.Value.BalanceQuantity -= reservation.
         Quantity;

         // record change
         ItemReservation change = new ItemReservation()
         { SKU = reservation.SKU, Quantity = reservation.
         Quantity, ReservedOn = DateTime.UtcNow };
         state.Value.Changes.Add(change);
         if (state.Value.Changes.Count > 10) state.Value.
         Changes.RemoveAt(0);

         await state.SaveAsync();

         // return current balance
         var result = new Item() {SKU = state.Value.SKU,
         Quantity= state.Value.BalanceQuantity};

         Console.WriteLine($"Reservation of {result.SKU} is
         now {result.Quantity}");

         return result;
     }
```

In the previous code snippet, we have the [HttpPost("reserve")] attribute instructing the Dapr runtime to invoke the ASP.Net controller via a POST.

The signature of the async Reserve method returns a result of the Task<ActionResult<Item>> type, with Item being a DTO type. The same type is accepted from clients as it used for the input parameter.

The state is requested, explicitly in the method code, asynchronously to the Dapr sidecar with `await daprClient.GetStateEntryAsync<ItemState>(StoreName, reservation.SKU)`, in which the two parameters are `storeName`, the name of the configured state store, and the `key` to look for in the state store.

Slightly different is the approach for the GET method implemented in `ReservationController.cs`:

```
[HttpGet("balance/{state}")]
public ActionResult<Item> Get([FromState(StoreName)]
StateEntry<ItemState> state)
{
    Console.WriteLine("Enter item retrieval");

    if (state.Value == null)
    {
        return this.NotFound();
    }
    var result = new Item() {SKU = state.Value.SKU,
    Quantity= state.Value.BalanceQuantity};

    Console.WriteLine($"Retrieved {result.SKU} is
    {result.Quantity}");

    return result;
    }
}
}
```

The `[HttpGet("balance/{state}")]` attribute influences the routing of requests to this method, which returns the item's DTO with `ActionResult<Item>`.

The state gets implicitly requested to Dapr via the `[FromState(StoreName)]` attribute of `StateEntry<ItemState> state`; an instance of the `StateEntry` type, with a `Value` of the `ItemState` type, is retrieved from the state store with the key passed in with `balance/{state}`.

It could be the case that there is no state registered for the submitted key, which can be evaluated by checking the `state.Value` property for null and, eventually, returning a `NotFound` result back to the caller.

As an example, the following interaction, directly reaching the ASP.NET service endpoint, returns the JSON payload of the serialized DTO:

```
GET http://localhost:5002/balance/cookie2 HTTP/1.1
{ "sku": "cookie2", "quantity": 52 }
```

For completeness, the following is the request to the Dapr state store endpoint:

```
GET http://localhost:5020/v1.0/state/reservationstore/cookie2
HTTP/1.1
```

For the time being, the `reservationstore` used by `reservation-service` is a state store component pointing to the local Redis; just by changing the component definition, it could switch to another, completely different store option.

So far, we have learned how to use `DaprClient` to manage state in our Dapr applications and how to configure a state store component.

In the next section, we will use a Cosmos DB as a store option and verify the implementation from Dapr's perspective.

Azure Cosmos DB as a state store

Instead of using the local Redis storage, we are going to leverage another Dapr state store option, **Azure Cosmos DB**, a globally distributed, multi-model database service.

The steps needed to associate the new state store are as follows:

1. Setting up Azure Cosmos DB
2. Configuring the state store
3. Testing the state store
4. Partitioning with Cosmos DB
5. Wrapping up

The application code of `reservation-store` will not be changed; we will only operate at the configuration of the state store component.

We start by setting up the Azure Cosmos DB resource.

Setting up Azure Cosmos DB

To create a Cosmos DB on Azure, please follow this guide in the Azure documentation: `https://docs.microsoft.com/en-us/azure/cosmos-db/how-to-manage-database-account`.

You should also take a look at the Dapr documentation for the same purpose: `https://docs.dapr.io/developing-applications/building-blocks/state-management/query-state-store/query-cosmosdb-store/`.

I created an Azure Cosmos DB account, a database named `state`, and then provisioned two containers, one for the `reservation-service` state store, and a second one for the `order-service` state store:

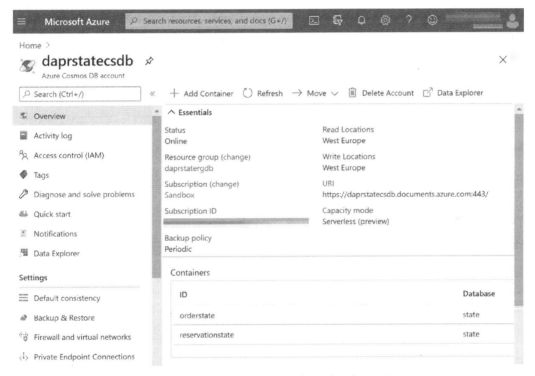

Figure 4.3 – Azure Cosmos DB configured with containers

I am using the serverless service tier of Cosmos DB, which bills only based on usage (it is the best option for a small application that doesn't have sustained traffic).

We are now ready to configure the state store component.

Configuring the state store

The Dapr component for a Cosmos DB is slightly different than the one for Redis, as you can see in the following code block:

```
apiVersion: dapr.io/v1alpha1
kind: Component
metadata:
  name: orderstore
spec:
  type: state.azure.cosmosdb
  metadata:
  - name: url
    value: https://daprstatecsdb.documents.azure.com:443/
  - name: masterKey
    value: <omitted>
  - name: database
    value: state
  - name: collection
    value: orderstate
```

The `url`, `database`, and `collection` match the provisioned Cosmos DB resources.

> **Important note**
>
> It is highly recommended that you do not keep secrets and credentials in configuration files and that you rely on the Dapr secret management feature instead.

During the `dapr run` launch sequence, we can look for evidence that the configured state stores are evaluated. From the lengthy output, the following is an excerpt:

```
PS C:\Repos\dapr-samples\chapter04> dapr run --app-id "order-
service" --app-port "5001" --dapr-grpc-port "50010" --dapr-
http-port "5010" --components-path "./components" -- dotnet
run --project ./sample.microservice.order/sample.microservice.
order.csproj --urls="http://+:5001"
```

The following is the corresponding output:

```
Starting Dapr with id order-service. HTTP Port: 5010. gRPC
Port: 50010
== DAPR == time="2020-09-19T11:06:22.6356595+02:00" level=info
msg="starting Dapr Runtime -- version 0.10.0 -- commit 6032dc2"
app_id=order-service instance=DB-SURFACEBOOK2 scope=dapr.
runtime type=log ver=0.10.0

== DAPR == time="2020-09-19T11:06:22.6356595+02:00" level=info
msg="log level set to: info" app_id=order-service instance=DB-
SURFACEBOOK2 scope=dapr.runtime type=log ver=0.10.0
...
== DAPR == time="2020-09-19T11:06:22.6536489+02:00" level=info
msg="found component reservationstore (state.azure.cosmosdb)"
app_id=order-service instance=DB-SURFACEBOOK2 scope=dapr.
runtime type=log ver=0.10.0

== DAPR == time="2020-09-19T11:06:22.6536489+02:00" level=info
msg="found component orderstore (state.azure.cosmosdb)" app_
id=order-service instance=DB-SURFACEBOOK2 scope=dapr.runtime
type=log ver=0.10.0
```

I added `--components-path "./components"` to specify the location of the `.yaml` file's components.

The following information messages tell us that `reservationstore (state.azure.cosmosdb)` and `orderstore (state.azure.cosmosdb)` have been correctly applied.

To avoid any confusion, `order-service` is going to use the `orderstore` state store, while `reservation-service` will leverage `reservationstore`. The `.yaml` files are located in the same folder.

The following diagram depicts the configuration change we applied:

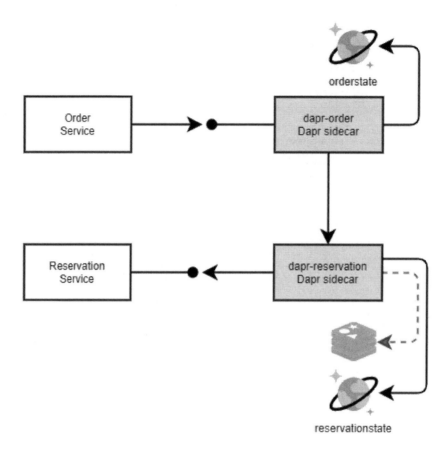

Figure 4.4 – Impact of a Dapr configurable state store

Figure 4.4 depicts the transparent change of the state store used by the `reservation-service` application from Redis to Azure Cosmos DB.

As we configured Cosmos DB as the state, and we have confirmation that the component is loaded by Dapr, it is time to test it!

Testing the state store

With `order-service` and `reservation-service` running and the state stores configured, it is time to test the services to appreciate how data is persisted on Azure Cosmos DB.

A POST command to the ASP.NET endpoint of the `order-service` endpoint will persist our new item in the state, in addition to invoking the `reservation-service` application:

```
POST http://localhost:5001/order HTTP/1.1
content-type: application/json

{
  "CustomerCode": "Davide",
  "Date": "2020-09-19T08:47:53.1224585Z",
  "Items": [
    {
      "ProductCode": "cookie4",
      "Quantity": 7
    },
    {
      "ProductCode": "bussola1",
      "Quantity": 6
    }
  ]
}
```

The following GET command invokes the `order-service` ASP.NET endpoint, which in turn invokes the Dapr state API:

```
GET http://localhost:5001/order/08ec11cc-7591-4702-bb4d-
7e86787b64fe
```

```
GET http://localhost:5010/v1.0/state/orderstore/08ec11cc-7591-
4702-bb4d-7e86787b64fe
```

While the Dapr application does rely on .NET SDK to get and save the state, it is often useful to check the persisted state directly by interacting with the Dapr API.

We can inspect how data is persisted as an item in Azure Cosmos DB, as shown in the following screenshot:

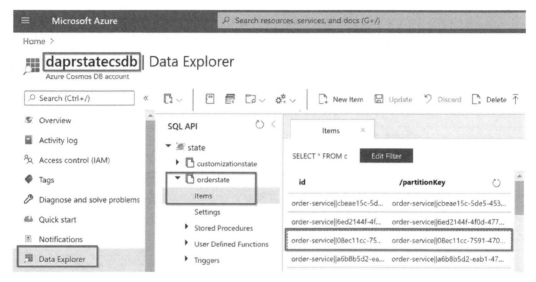

Figure 4.5 – Data Explorer in Azure Cosmos DB

As shown in *Figure 4.5*, we can reach the data persisted by the Dapr state with the following steps:

1. Open the **Data Explorer** from the navigation pane.

2. Select the database and the relevant container.

3. Browse the items.

4. Examine the record content containing the Dapr state:

```
1   {
2       "id": "order-service||08ec11cc-7591-4702-bb4d-7e86787b64fe",
3       "value": {
4           "CreatedOn": "2020-09-19T12:28:19.2450723Z",
5           "UpdatedOn": "2020-09-19T12:28:19.2451555Z",
6           "Order": {
7               "Date": "2020-09-19T08:47:53.1224585Z",
8               "Id": "08ec11cc-7591-4702-bb4d-7e86787b64fe",
9               "CustomerCode": "Davide",
10              "Items": [
11                  {
12                      "ProductCode": "cookie4",
13                      "Quantity": 7
14                  },
15                  {
16                      "ProductCode": "bussola1",
17                      "Quantity": 6
18                  }
19              ]
20          }
21      },
22      "partitionKey": "order-service||08ec11cc-7591-4702-bb4d-7e86787b64fe",
23      "_rid": "h+ETAOzuFXEMAAAAAAAAAA==",
24      "_self": "dbs/h+ETAA==/colls/h+ETAOzuFXE=/docs/h+ETAOzuFXEMAAAAAAAAAA==/",
25      "_etag": "\"18006115-0000-0d00-0000-5f65f9630000\"",
26      "_attachments": "attachments/",
27      "_ts": 1600518499
28  }
```

Figure 4.6 – Item in Azure Cosmos DB Data Explorer

As shown in *Figure 4.6*, the state is persisted as JSON, with the main payload in the `value` field and item `id` being the Dapr state key composed with the pattern `<application Id>||<state key>`.

We learned firsthand how the Cosmo DB Dapr's state store persists our application state in the database, so let's now investigate how the key and distribution of records are correlated.

Partitioning with Cosmos DB

Partitioning enable Azure Cosmos DB to scale individual containers in a database, as items grouped along the partition key in logical partitions are then positioned in physical partitions: it is one of the most relevant concepts that Cosmo DB adopts in terms of offering a high level of performance.

By default, the Dapr state key is used as the `partitionKey` for each item in the Cosmos DB container. Considering that the Dapr state API always uses the key to read and write data from Cosmos DB, it should be a good choice in most cases.

In case you need to influence the `partitionKey`, you can specify it with the `metadata` parameter while interacting the state object. As an example, let's see the following code:

```
var metadata = new Dictionary<string,string>();
metadata.Add("partitionKey","something_else");
await state.SaveAsync(metadata: metadata);
```

In cases where we modified our `order-service` Dapr application to adopt a different partitioning scheme, this would be the persisted document in Cosmos DB:

```
{
    "id": "order-service||f5a34876-2737-4e8f-aba5-
    002a4e1ab0cc",
    "value": {
        "CreatedOn": "2020-09-19T11:15:20.7463172Z",
        "UpdatedOn": "2020-09-19T11:15:20.746392Z",
        "Order": {
            "Date": "2020-09-19T08:47:53.1224585Z",
            "Id": "f5a34876-2737-4e8f-aba5-002a4e1ab0cc",
            "CustomerCode": "Davide",
            "Items": [
                {
                    "ProductCode": "cookie4",
                    "Quantity": 7
                },
                {
                    "ProductCode": "bussola1",
                    "Quantity": 6
                }
            ]
        }
    },
    "partitionKey": "something_else",
    "_rid": "h+ETAOzuFXELAAAAAAAAAA==",
```

```
    "_self": "dbs/h+ETAA==/colls/h+ETAOzuFXE=/docs/
    h+ETAOzuFXELAAAAAAAAAA==/",
    "_etag": "\"1800590c-0000-0d00-0000-5f65e8480000\"",
    "_attachments": "attachments/",
    "_ts": 1600514120
}
```

In the preceding code snippet, you can see "partitionKey": "something_else" and how it differs from the "id": "order-service||f5a34876-2737-4e8f-aba5-002a4e1ab0cc" key, being influenced by the metadata parameter in the SaveAsync method.

In most cases, the default approach to partitioning should be fine, but now you know how to control it.

Using Azure Cosmos DB as a state store for Dapr does not prevent us from using it for additional scenarios, as we will learn next.

Wrapping up

As we were able to prove, Dapr does influence the data persisted in the state store with its minimalistic approach. Apart from the key/value, the payload is untouched and consumable, just like any other JSON document.

This opens up an additional scenario: what if I need to search for orders submitted to order-service, which contains a specific item by ProductCode? This is not information that we can search for using the Dapr runtime, as you can see here:

```
SELECT c.id FROM c WHERE ARRAY_CONTAINS(c["value"]["Order"].
Items, {"ProductCode": "bussola2"}, true)
```

The query shown, executed on the container used as the state store by order-service, will return a list of item IDs, including the following:

```
[
    {
        "id": "order-service||bbc1f16a-c7e3-48c3-91fb-
        b2175acfc299"
    },
    {
        "id": "order-service||91705574-df80-4844-af5f-
        66877c436e9b"
    },
    {
        "id": "order-service||ac1e173e-fe4e-476f-b6f6-
```

```
             e9615a49f47b"
      }
   ]
```

A method in our Dapr application could perform the query directly against the Azure Cosmos DB using the native .NET SDK to obtain the state key from the ID. As we know, the Dapr state key is composed as `<App ID>||<state key>`, and we can derive the orders in the scope of our search: `order.id bbc1f16a-c7e3-48c3-91fb-b2175acfc299`, `91705574-df80-4844-af5f-66877c436e9b`, and `ac1e173e-fe4e-476f-b6f6-e9615a49f47b` are the ones containing the `ProductCode` we were looking for.

This is not information that we could obtain with a query via the Dapr runtime to the API.

Any requirement outside the scope of the Dapr state API can be approached natively by interacting with, in this scenario, Cosmos DB.

External manipulation of the state should always be avoided, but there is nothing preventing you from reading it.

We have now completed our exploration of a powerful database, Azure Cosmos DB, used in Dapr as a state store.

Summary

In this chapter, we introduced the state management API provided by Dapr and learned how an ASP.NET service can leverage it via the .NET SDKs. We also appreciated the flexibility offered by Dapr to developers and operators in terms of configuring and modifying the state stores.

By testing the Dapr state management with local Redis and then with the cloud-based Azure Cosmos DB, we proved how easy it is not only to move the state outside of a stateful microservice, but also to shift from one persistence technology to another simply via a configuration change. We have learned how to build an application with Dapr that is capable of using a state store to support a specific context. For example, to accommodate different customer requirements.

In the next chapter, we will discuss a flexible and scalable approach to communicating between Dapr applications.

5
Publish and Subscribe

Publish/subscribe is the messaging pattern supported by Dapr to enable decoupled interactions between microservices.

In this chapter, you will understand the benefits of the publish/subscribe messaging-based pattern and how to implement it in your Dapr applications.

These are the main topics of this chapter:

- Using the publish and subscribe pattern in Dapr
- Using **Azure Service Bus** in Dapr
- Implementing a saga pattern

Before we delve into the implementation details of publish and subscribe in Dapr, an overview of the pattern is necessary.

Technical requirements

The code for this sample can be found on GitHub at `https://github.com/PacktPublishing/Practical-Microservices-with-Dapr-and-.NET/tree/main/chapter05`.

In this chapter, the working area for scripts and code is expected to be `<repository path>\chapter05\`. In my local environment, it is `C:\Repos\dapr-samples\chapter05`.

Please refer to the *Setting up Dapr* section in *Chapter 1*, *Introducing Dapr*, for a complete guide on the tools needed to develop with Dapr and work with the samples.

Using the publish and subscribe pattern in Dapr

In microservice architectures, the **publish and subscribe** pattern (also known as **publish/subscribe** or **pub/sub**) is widely adopted to facilitate the creation of a decoupled communication channel between different parts of the application.

The sender (the publisher) of messages/events is both unaware of which microservices would consume them and at which point in time they would do it.

On the receiving end (the subscriber) of this pattern, the microservice expresses an interest for the information shared as messages/events, by subscribing to a specific set of information types, or topics (to use a better term). (Note that it is not forced to consume the complete stream of messages; it will be able to distill the relevant information from the rest.)

With a similar perspective, a subscriber, too, is not aware of the location and status of the publisher:

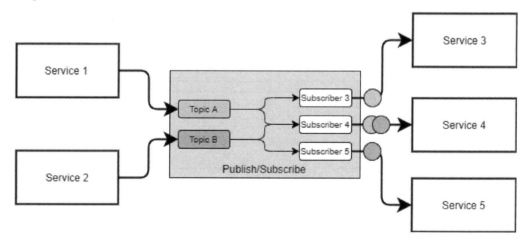

Figure 5.1 – Publish/subscribe pattern

In *Figure 5.1*, you can see the publish and subscribe pattern in action: services publish messages specifying the topic – this could be of interest to other services that subscribe to one or many topics.

Over time, more subscribers can be added, with no impact on the publisher.

The pub/sub pattern is often pitted against the service-to-service invocation approach: the first offers a separation in location and time between the request and its processing, while the latter offers a predictable interaction and expectation of response time.

With publish/subscribe, it's more complex to implement closed loops of request/response, as it's not meant for this style of interaction; on the contrary, the pattern enables each microservice to operate at its own pace, scaling independently and evolving autonomously.

In a service-to-service interaction, the microservices are well aware of each other, as they share an agreement (or contract) on not only the payload schema but also on the API surface, and should aim to sustain the pace of the fastest component. Being so closely coupled brings the benefit of simpler interactions with shorter request/response cycles, as there are no intermediaries.

In the discussion of the pub/sub pattern, it might be useful to disambiguate between the concepts of message and event: they both define a piece of information shared between systems, but a message is usually used to pass the request to continue processing elsewhere, while an event brings the news that something already happened to which a reaction is possible.

Let's use the example common to all our samples so far, that is, our cookie-selling e-commerce site:

- An example of an event could be the signaling of a customer accessing our e-commerce site or the expiration time of their shopping cart.

- An example of a message could the request to compensate an activity, for example, to void the impact of an order, sent from one microservice to another, previously performed via direct service invocation, asynchronously but as soon as possible.

Apart from the conceptual differences and use cases, both messages and events are equally supported by the publish/subscribe building block of Dapr.

An important role in a publish/subscribe pattern is played by the messaging system, which is responsible for the ingestion, safe storage, and consumption of messages, interacting with publishers and subscribers over standard protocols.

The externalization of responsibilities of a messaging system, be it a hosted software package or a messaging system as a service, as commonly provided by most major cloud vendors, is a common pattern of microservice architectures.

Dapr currently supports integration with the following messaging systems:

- **Azure Service Bus (ASB)**
- Azure Event Hubs
- NATS
- Kafka
- GCP Pub/Sub
- MQTT
- RabbitMQ
- Redis Streams
- Hazelcast

By default, Dapr enables Redis as a pub/sub component, also acting as a state store, in the self-hosted hosting mode.

As a pluggable runtime, Dapr enables the configuration of multiple pub/sub components to be used by the same application.

A Dapr application or client can interact with the pub/sub component via the Dapr API: a simple `POST` request to the Dapr local endpoint exposed by the sidecar with the `http://localhost:<daprPort>/v1.0/publish/<pubsubname>/<topic>` structure would publish data to other Dapr applications subscribing to the same topic named `<topic>` via the configured component named `<pubsubname>`.

In addition to the Dapr API, the Dapr .NET SDK simplifies publishing messages by abstracting the interaction with the API, as well as subscribing to topics and receiving messages.

The delivery of messages to subscribing Dapr applications is guaranteed *at least once*: the runtime takes care of all the complexities and specifics of the messaging system, with no need for additional libraries, and guarantees the message is going to be delivered at least once to any of the Dapr application's instances positively replying to the Dapr API, with an HTTP result code of `200` or without raising exceptions.

The *at least once* delivery mechanism in Dapr enables your application to have competing consumers: the messages relevant to the subscribed topics will be split among all the running instances of that specific Dapr application. On the other hand, be cautious that if your code needs to make sure that the message will be processed only once, it is your code's responsibility to avoid duplicates.

As we have learned the basic concepts of messaging in Dapr with publish/subscribe, we are now prepared to apply using ASB as a cloud message broker with Dapr in the next section.

Using Azure Service Bus in Dapr

To introduce the pub/sub building block of Dapr with the ASB implementation, we will develop, in C#, a prototype of a collaboration between some .NET microservices.

This is what we would like to accomplish:

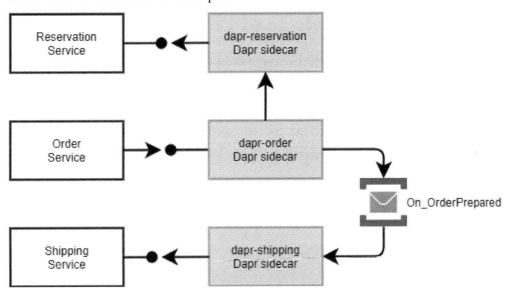

Figure 5.2 – Publish/subscribe in Dapr with ASB

In *Figure 5.2*, we have the **Order** service interacting with the **Reservation** service via service-to-service invocation, and with the **Shipping** service via pub/sub: this is the portion we are going to develop.

In the chapter05 folder, you will find many projects; for now, we will focus on order-service (sample.microservice.order) and shipping-service (sample.microservice.shipping).

> **Important note: projects and solution**
>
> I created samples with several C# projects grouped in a solution, with separate projects for **data transfer objects (DTOs)** and a common library for constants and so on referenced by both the service and client projects.
>
> My intention was to organize the assets in a way that would be easy to consume for you: two microservices could also agree on the JSON format exchanged between the parties and avoid DTOs and references.

To implement the publish/subscribe pattern, we are going to follow these steps:

1. Subscribe a topic.

2. Configure a pub/sub component.

3. Publish to a topic.

4. Inspect the messages.

The first step to build our code is to instrument a Dapr service to subscribe a pub/sub topic. In the following sections, we will see how to go about these steps.

Subscribing a topic

I created the `sample.microservice.shipping` project and then referenced the DTO project via the `dotnet` CLI:

```
PS C:\Repos\dapr-samples\chapter05> dotnet new classlib -o
"sample.microservice.dto.shipping"
```
```
PS C:\Repos\dapr-samples\chapter05> dotnet new webapi -o
"sample.microservice.shipping"
```

Let's first examine the `Startup.cs` configuration of this ASP.NET project code: it will have some differences to support pub/sub:

```
public void Configure(IApplicationBuilder app,
IWebHostEnvironment env)
{
    if (env.IsDevelopment())
    {
        app.UseDeveloperExceptionPage();
    }

    app.UseRouting();
```

```
        app.UseCloudEvents();

    app.UseAuthorization();

    app.UseEndpoints(endpoints =>
    {
        endpoints.MapSubscribeHandler();
        endpoints.MapControllers();
    });
    }
```

The changes to the `Configure` method are mainly the following:

- The call to `endpoints.MapSubscribeHandler()` registers an endpoint that the Dapr runtime in the sidecar will invoke, to become aware of the topics our microservice subscribes to. Without this statement, we would not be able to receive messages from Dapr.

- We use `app.UseCloudEvents` to support the requests with `Content-Type` `application/cloudevents+json` so that the **CloudEvents** payload can be accessed directly.

We will now move on to decorating our ASP.NET controller to subscribe to a Dapr pub/sub topic.

The following is the method signature of `ShippingController.cs` in the `sample.microservice.shipping` project:

```
namespace sample.microservice.shipping.Controllers
{
    [ApiController]
    public class ShippingController : ControllerBase
    {
        public const string StoreName = "shippingstore";
        public const string PubSub = "commonpubsub";

        [Topic(PubSub, Topics.OrderPreparedTopicName)]
        [HttpPost("ship")]
        public async Task<ActionResult<Guid>> ship(Shipment
        orderShipment, [FromServices] DaprClient daprClient)
        {
            Console.WriteLine("Enter shipment start");

            var state = await daprClient.
            GetStateEntryAsync<ShippingState>(StoreName,
```

```
                  orderShipment.OrderId.ToString());
        state.Value ??= new ShippingState() {OrderId =
        orderShipment.OrderId, ShipmentId = Guid.NewGuid()
        };

        await state.SaveAsync();

        var result = state.Value.ShipmentId;
        Console.WriteLine($"Shipment of orderId
        {orderShipment.OrderId} completed with id
        {result}");

        return New OkResult();
    }
  }
}
```

By decorating the method with the `[Topic(<pubsub component>, <topic name>]` attribute, I instructed Dapr to subscribe to a topic in the pub/sub component, and to invoke this method if a message arrives.

Before we can publish any messages, we need to configure Dapr.

Configuring a pub/sub component

Our objective is to configure a Dapr component to support the pub/sub building block.

First, we need an external messaging system: we could have used the Redis stream made available by the Dapr setup.

Instead, we are going to create an ASB namespace and leverage it in Dapr for some good reasons (and a strong personal preference by myself).

At this stage in developing our sample, we are running in self-hosted mode. Starting from *Chapter 8, Deploying to Kubernetes*, we will use Kubernetes mode in Dapr: I think that reducing the breadth of changes to the Dapr mode while keeping the components constant helps to focus on what is relevant. In addition, the effort of keeping Redis as a reliable messaging store in Kubernetes is significant and beyond the scope of this book.

The following is its definition from the documentation at `https://docs.microsoft.com/en-us/azure/service-bus-messaging/service-bus-messaging-overview`:

"Microsoft Azure Service Bus is a fully managed enterprise integration message broker. Service Bus can decouple applications and services. Service Bus offers a reliable and secure platform for asynchronous transfer of data and state."

You can find detailed instructions on how to create an ASB namespace at `https://docs.microsoft.com/en-us/azure/service-bus-messaging/service-bus-create-namespace-portal`, including how to obtain the connection string we will use later in the chapter.

As developers (or operators), we do not have the responsibility of provisioning the ASB topics and subscriptions, nor to provide the deployment scripts: Dapr will take care of dynamically creating the topics that applications will publish to and the corresponding subscriptions.

In the `\components` folder, we create a `pubsub.yaml` file with the following structure:

```
apiVersion: dapr.io/v1alpha1
kind: Component
metadata:
  name: commonpubsub
  namespace: default
spec:
  type: pubsub.azure.servicebus
  metadata:
  - name: connectionString
    value: … omitted … # Required.
```

Each Dapr component has its metadata configuration; for the `pubsub.azure.servicebus` component type, you can find the details at `https://docs.dapr.io/developing-applications/building-blocks/pubsub/howto-publish-subscribe/`.

How can we know that our service correctly registered the subscription to the topic? By launching `shipping-service`, we can inspect the Dapr output:

```
PS C:\Repos\dapr-samples\chapter05> dapr run --app-id
"shipping-service" --app-port "5005" --dapr-grpc-port "50050"
--da
pr-http-port "5050" --components-path "./components" -- dotnet
run --project ./sample.microservice.shipping/sample.micro
service.shipping.csproj --urls="http://+:5005"
Starting Dapr with id shipping-service. HTTP Port: 5050. gRPC
Port: 50050
… omitted …
== DAPR == time="2020-09-26T19:25:40.7256112+02:00" level=info
```

```
msg="found component commonpubsub (pubsub.azure.servicebu
s)" app_id=shipping-service instance=DB-SURFACEBOOK2
scope=dapr.runtime type=log ver=0.10.0

... omitted ...

Updating metadata for app command: dotnet run --project ./
sample.microservice.shipping/sample.microservice.shipping.cspr
oj --urls=http://+:5005
You're up and running! Both Dapr and your app logs will appear
here.
```

From the Dapr output, we can see that the `commonpubsub` (`pubsub.azure.servicebus`) component has been found and set up.

What happened to the messaging system ASB now that we defined a pub/sub component and a subscriber?

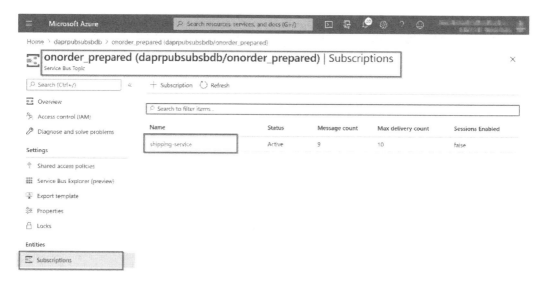

Figure 5.3 – ASB subscriptions of a topic

As you can see in *Figure 5.3*, Dapr created a topic named `onorder_prepared` in the ASB namespace, with a subscription named `shipping-service`.

The next step is to learn how to publish messages to a pub/sub topic in Dapr.

Publishing to a topic

Any Dapr application can invoke the Dapr runtime reaching the HTTP API, via the SDK or with the Dapr CLI.

We are going to see how the Dapr CLI works:

```
dapr publish --pubsub commonpubsub -t OnOrder_Prepared -d
'{\"OrderId\": \"6271e8f3-f99f-4e03-98f7-6f136dbb8de8\"}'
```

The dapr publish command lets me send data to a topic, via a pub/sub component.

It is time to verify whether the message has been received.

From the shipping-service terminal window, we can see that the message has been received and processed:

```
== APP == Enter shipment start

== APP == Shipment of orderId 6271e8f3-f99f-4e03-98f7-
6f136dbb8de8 completed with id 53c3cc5c-0193-412b-97e9-
f82f3e0d2f8
0
```

We found the feedback that the publish/subscribe is working as expected from the service output, but how can we inspect the messages?

Inspecting the messages

By playing around with dapr publish, you should soon realize that even the added latency between your development environment and the Azure cloud is very small, from a human perspective: each message that is sent is promptly received by the Dapr microservice.

The ability of a publisher and subscriber to operate independently is one of the major benefits of the pub/sub pattern: we will leverage it to facilitate our learning of Dapr.

As long as there are other Dapr applications running in the local development environment, the messages can be published successfully even if you terminate the shipping-service Dapr application.

With the subscriber shipping-service application inactive, we can enqueue some messages by publishing with the Dapr CLI and have the chance to inspect them.

By leveraging the **Service Bus Explorer** feature of ASB via the Azure portal, we can see whether there are pending messages in the subscription:

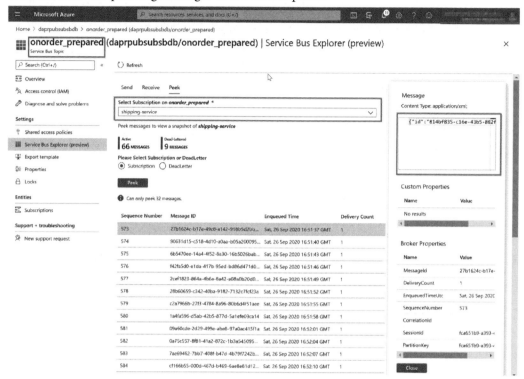

Figure 5.4 – Service Bus Explorer view of a Dapr service subscription

As you can see in *Figure. 5.4*, we managed to get several messages in the subscription. With the **Peek** function, the messages can be inspected without reading them; by selecting one of the messages, we can access the payload.

By inspecting the messages persisted into the auditing subscription, we can see the CloudEvents format being used:

```
{
    "id": "4e2f90d0-56ec-4939-badf-9ffd034199cd",
    "source": "console",
    "type": "com.dapr.event.sent",
    "specversion": "1.0",
    "datacontenttype": "application/json",
    "data": {
        "OrderId": "08ec11cc-7591-4702-bb4d-7e86787b64fe"
    },
    "subject": "00-1f0f371b9b52924fbc5772d328c40af5-
```

```
f8abbfbf1fbc0a42-01",
    "topic": "OnOrder_Prepared",
    "pubsubname": "commonpubsub"
}
```

The information we sent via the `dapr publish` command is in the `data` field of the message payload, and thanks to the changes we applied in the `Startup.cs` file of our ASP.NET project, our code can deal with only the relevant portion of the CloudEvents payload.

CloudEvents is a **Cloud Native Computing Foundation** (**CNCF**) specification for describing event data: it has been adopted by Dapr to format the messages exchanged via pub/sub. See `https://cloudevents.io/` for more information on the specification.

We had our first experience with the publish and subscribe component of Dapr: instead of service-to-service invocation, we interacted with a Dapr application by publishing a message to a topic, relying on an external messaging system such as ASB.

In the next section, we will leverage the Dapr publish/subscribe building block for a more complex pattern.

Implementing a saga pattern

As we learned about how the publish and subscribe pattern is implemented in Dapr, we can now apply this knowledge to building a more complex scenario, leveraging the saga design pattern for an e-commerce order system.

There are many authoritative sources that discuss the saga pattern in detail; among them, I suggest reading `https://docs.microsoft.com/en-us/azure/architecture/reference-architectures/saga/saga` and `https://vasters.com/archive/Sagas.html`, since it is not in the scope of this book to add anything to an already-rich conversation on the subject.

In a microservice architecture, a business activity (for instance, processing an order) could be divided into smaller tasks, carried out by a sequence of microservices interacting with each other.

We learned that while a microservice gains a lot of benefits by isolating its state, a consequence of this autonomy is that distributed transactions are not conceivable over disparate combinations of databases and libraries. A distributed transaction in this scenario would probably be a bad idea as the transactional context could grow in complexity over time, with more microservices being added or evolving, and have a longer duration: a microservice could not always be available to process the same activity at the same time.

To overcome this reality, a microservice should focus on its scope of responsibility, using local transactions on its own state store/database, publish a message or signal an event to notify the completion of its part of the overall activity, and be able to compensate it with a transaction to reverse the effects on its state, in case the overall sequence of transactions (the saga) is considered as failed.

In a nutshell, a saga pattern comes into play in microservice architectures to orchestrate data consistency between the many state stores.

The following figure shows an example of a saga pattern:

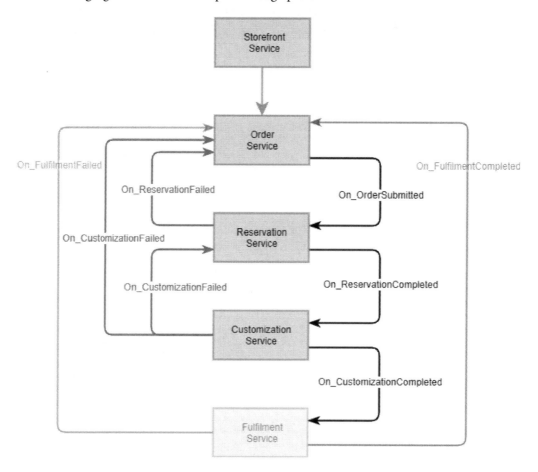

Figure 5.5 – Saga pattern with Dapr

In the context of our cookie-selling e-commerce scenario, this is how we will structure the saga for our ordering activity, also depicted in *Figure. 5.5*:

- An order is submitted (likely from a web frontend) to `order-service`, which registers and publishes it to the `OnOrder_Submitted` topic. `order-service` does not verify the availability of items at the ordered quantity at this stage of the sequence: it is far more likely that if an item landed in the shopping cart, it is available.

   `order-service` subscribes to many other topics which signal that, because of irreversible conditions, the order is canceled. As other microservices rely on `order-service` to know the status of an order, the responsibility to keep an order's status up to date lies with the `order-service`.

- `reservation-service` subscribes to the `OnOrder_Submitted` topic to learn about new orders and affect the item's available quantities, before sending a message to the `OnReservation_Completed` topic. If any of the items' quantities in the order could not be allocated, it compensates for the already-allocated items by reversing the effect on the available quantity, before publishing the message to the `OnReservation_Failed` topic. By subscribing to the `OnCustomization_failed` topic, `reservation-service` will attempt to compensate the available quantity for the items not already customized, which will be discarded as they cannot be sold to anyone else.

- The other microservice, `customization-service`, operates in a similar fashion: by publishing messages on the `OnCustomization_failed` topic to signal the next steps to continue or compensate, and by subscribing to the `OnReservation_Completed` topic, informing the completion of previous steps in the saga.

- As it would not offer a new perspective on the saga pattern, for brevity, the `fulfilment-service` microservice is out of the scope of this sample.

There are several steps to implement the saga:

1. Publish messages to Dapr.
2. Subscribe to a Dapr topic.
3. Test the saga pattern.

The first step to build our code is to instrument `order-service` to publish a message to the intended topic.

Publishing messages to Dapr

After we configure each ASP.NET web API project to support subscriber handlers and process CloudEvents, as we did in the previous section, we are ready to publish our first message via the Dapr ASP.NET SDK. It's as simple as this:

```
await daprClient.PublishEventAsync<Order>(PubSub, common.
Topics.OrderSubmittedTopicName, order);
```

Let's understand the preceding code:

- The preceding code invokes the `PublishEventAsync<T>` method of the instance of type `DaprClient` that our ASP.NET controller gained access to, via dependency injection: `DaprClient` is our .NET gateway to all of Dapr's building blocks.

- The first parameter is `pubsubname`: it should match the `commonpubsub` we specified in the `.yaml` file we placed in the `\components` folder. Our microservice can use multiple pub/sub components at the same time.

- The second parameter is `topicName`, which will influence the routing of our messages and will translate to the ASB topic name itself.

- The third parameter is `data`: the message payload.

> **Important note**
>
> This sample code is simple and straightforward: it considers compensating activities and simulates conditions of error in the business logic, but does not offer proper exception handling. You should invest your efforts into elaborating this on your own, as both expected and unexpected conditions should be evaluated to decide whether it makes sense to retry, because of transient errors, or fail and compensate.

In the next section, we will subscribe to the appropriate publish/subscribe topic.

Subscribing to a Dapr topic

As we learned in a previous section, *Subscribing a topic*, an ASP.NET controller method signature can be decorated with the `[Topic]` attribute to subscribe to messages from the topic. Refer to the following code:

```
[Topic(PubSub, common.Topics.CustomizationFailedTopicName)]
        [HttpPost(common.Topics.CustomizationFailedTopicName)]
        public async Task<ActionResult<Guid>>
```

```
OnCustomizationFailed(OrderCustomization customization,
[FromServices] DaprClient daprClient)

{
… omitted …
}
```

To leverage the Dapr ASP.NET integration, the controller's method should also have `route attribute`: it might seem counterintuitive at first, but the Dapr runtime will invoke this method once it receives a message from the topic.

An important point of attention is on the ASP.NET controller's outcome. As documented in the Dapr documentation at `https://docs.dapr.io/reference/api/pubsub_api/#expected-http-response`, the HTTP result does influence how the Dapr runtime handles the message passed to the subscriber. Let's examine a few possible outputs:

- An `HTTP 200` response with an empty payload, or with a `status` key and `"SUCCESS"` value in a JSON payload, informs the Dapr runtime that the message has been successfully processed by the subscriber.

- An `HTTP 200` response with a JSON payload, a `status` key and `RETRY` value, informs Dapr that the message must be retried: this is helpful if your microservice encounters a transient error.

  Other responses can inform Dapr to log a warning or error, to drop or retry the message.

All the microservices have been instructed to publish and subscribe to their messages: it's time to test the overall scenario.

Testing the saga pattern

Via the Dapr CLI, we can launch the three microservices in the scope of the saga implementation from different terminal windows:

1. The originating order payload evolved to include special requests for customization:

   ```
   POST http://localhost:5001/order HTTP/1.1
   content-type: application/json

   {
     "CustomerCode": "Davide",
     "Items": [
       … omitted …
   ```

```
    ],
    "SpecialRequests" : [
      {
        "CustomizationId" : "08ffffcc-7591-4702-ffff-
        fff6787bfffe",
        "Scope":
        {
          "ProductCode": "crazycookie",
          "Quantity": 1
        }
      }
    ]
}
```

2. The order is immediately submitted: the `order-service` microservice communicates via pub/sub with the other microservices, not via service-to-service invocation, so it's not slowed down by their processing time:

```
== APP == Submitted order 17ecdc67-880e-4f34-92cb-
ed13abbd1e68
```

3. The `reservation-service` microservice allocates the item quantity:

```
== APP == Reservation in 17ecdc67-880e-4f34-92cb-
ed13abbd1e68 of rockiecookie for 4, balance 76
== APP == Reservation in 17ecdc67-880e-4f34-92cb-
ed13abbd1e68 of bussola8 for 7, balance 1
== APP == Reservation in 17ecdc67-880e-4f34-92cb-
ed13abbd1e68 of crazycookie for 2, balance 19
== APP == Reservation in 17ecdc67-880e-4f34-92cb-
ed13abbd1e68 completed
```

4. The `customization-service` microservice is ready to receive special requests for customizing the cookies. Unfortunately, the customization of the `crazycookie` SKU is almost certain to fail:

```
== APP == Customization in 17ecdc67-880e-4f34-92cb-
ed13abbd1e68 of crazycookie for 1 failed
```

```
== DAPR == time="2020-10-05T21:36:09.1056547+02:00"
level=error msg="non-retriable error returned from
app while processing pub/sub event ca651732-3a86-
442c-a16c-22cde9f10669: {\"type\":\"https://tools.
ietf.org/html/rfc7231#section-6.5.4\",\"title\":\"Not
Found\",\"status\":404,\"traceId\":\"00-
```

```
d361dfa4708d341f7c455c36f9c55fe5-caefa84996088f47-01\"}.
status code returned: 404" app_id=customization-service
instance=DB-SURFACEBOOK2 scope=dapr.runtime type=log
ver=0.11.1
```

`customization-service`, in fact, fails and it publishes a message in `OnCustomization_failed` to notify the saga participants. As you can see, we received an output from the application and from Dapr as well: in this case, the `customization-service` code sample returned a response to inform that, while something unexpected happened, the message should not be retried as the condition of error is considered unrecoverable.

5. `reservation-service` also has the goal of compensating for the failed order customization by releasing the reserved quantities for all the items that have *not* already been customized, and therefore are still sellable.

    As `reservation-service` subscribes to the `OnCustomizationFailed` topic, it is ready to do so:

```
== APP == Reservation in 17ecdc67-880e-4f34-92cb-
ed13abbd1e68 of rockiecookie for -4, balance 80
== APP == Reservation in 17ecdc67-880e-4f34-92cb-
ed13abbd1e68 of bussola8 for -7, balance 8
== APP == Reservation in 17ecdc67-880e-4f34-92cb-
ed13abbd1e68 of crazycookie for -1, balance 20
== APP == Acknowledged customization failed for order
17ecdc67-880e-4f34-92cb-ed13abbd1e68
```

    As an additional note, in the `ReservationController.cs` file, to compensate for the reservation on the item quantities, the **Language Integrated Query (LINQ)** technology has been used to calculate it. As this is not in this book's scope, I encourage you to go read and learn more on the topic from the documentation at `https://docs.microsoft.com/en-us/dotnet/csharp/programming-guide/concepts/linq/`.

6. `order-service` subscribes to the `OnCustomizationFailed` topic too: if we look at the ASB namespace in the Azure portal, we should see two subscriptions on the `OnCustomizationFailed` topic.

    Also, this microservice receives this message on the customization failure:

```
== APP == Acknowledged customization failed for order
17ecdc67-880e-4f34-92cb-ed13abbd1e68
```

With this brief sequence of traces, we were able to implement and appreciate the simplicity and power of the saga pattern with Dapr.

Summary

In this chapter, we learned how to adopt the publish/subscribe building block of Dapr to decouple the communication between microservices, in a way that is far more efficient than we achieved with service-to-service direct invocation, but not without additional efforts.

We figured out how to configure the publish/subscribe component with Azure Service Bus and how to use the Dapr .NET SDK to instruct the ASP.NET controllers to publish and subscribe messages.

Finally, we discussed using the saga design pattern to tackle the complexity of distributed data consistency, without resorting to distributed transactions, and implemented it in our sample scenario.

In the next chapter, we will explore the resource-binding building block to interact with external services and events.

6
Resource Bindings

The focus of this chapter is on **resource bindings** in Dapr: a convenient and pluggable approach to invoking external systems from Dapr microservices and triggering Dapr applications based on external events.

These are the main topics we will explore in this chapter:

- Learning how to use Dapr bindings
- Using Twilio output bindings in Dapr
- Ingesting data in C# with the Azure Event Hubs input binding

Learning about Dapr resource bindings is important in the scope of developing new solutions and to improve existing ones. While the pub/sub pattern we explored in *Chapter 5, Publish and Subscribe*, is helpful in orchestrating asynchronous communication between Dapr applications, the knowledge we get from resource bindings in this chapter will bring interoperability into our solution.

The very first step in this journey is to learn more about Dapr resource bindings.

Technical requirements

The code for this sample can be found on GitHub at `https://github.com/ PacktPublishing/Practical-Microservices-with-Dapr-and-.NET/ tree/main/chapter06`.

In this chapter, the working area for scripts and code is expected to be `<repository path>\chapter06\`. In my local environment, it is `C:\Repos\dapr-samples\chapter06`.

Please refer to the *Setting up Dapr* section in *Chapter 1, Introducing Dapr*, for a complete guide on the tools needed to develop with Dapr and work with the samples.

Learning how to use Dapr bindings

In previous chapters, we devoted most of our attention to the Dapr architecture, and how to use its building blocks to facilitate communication between microservices in the context of the Dapr environment.

Here, we will see that with Dapr's service-to-service building blocks, we can directly invoke another microservice as the Dapr runtime takes care of routing requests to their destination and handling retries, among other benefits.

By managing the state, Dapr lifts from our microservice the responsibility of maintaining the plumbing code and the libraries necessary to interact with a persistence layer.

By supporting the publish/subscribe pattern, Dapr enables microservices to communicate in a loosely coupled fashion and allows our overall architecture to grow in complexity, minimizing the impact on existing portions of code.

All these building blocks focus inward, into our microservices, although often, the architecture is not completely isolated as there is a need to reach external systems outside of our microservices, whether it is to receive data, react to external events, or communicate events. Sometimes, the need could be as simple as to leverage a specific technology or cloud service from our microservices, such as notifications via Azure SignalR or AWS SNS.

The Dapr **resource bindings** building block can be used as **output** or **input** for our Dapr applications.

As an example, these are a few of the currently available output bindings, allowing a Dapr application to execute a specific action on the resource:

- HTTP
- Kafka
- MQTT
- RabbitMQ
- Twilio

- Twitter
- Azure: Blob Storage, Event Hubs, Cosmos DB, Service Bus, SignalR, Queue Storage, Event Grid
- AWS: DynamoDB, S3, SNS, SQS, Kinesis
- GCP: Cloud Pub/Sub, Storage Bucket

Some of the available input bindings, allowing a Dapr application to be invoked based on an event raised by the resource, are as follows:

- Cron
- Kafka
- MQTT
- RabbitMQ
- Twitter
- Azure: Event Hubs, Service Bus, Queue Storage, Event Grid
- AWS: SQS, Kinesis
- GCP: Cloud Pub/Sub

To use a binding in Dapr, first it must be configured as a component. Let's see how to configure one of the simplest blocks: the Cron input binding.

Configuring a Cron input binding

In the local development environment, the `.yaml` files must be located in the folder specified in the Dapr CLI, `dapr run --app-id "<application>" --components-path "./components"`. Each Dapr application could have a different path but, as some components are used by several Dapr applications in this book's samples, I will keep all `.yaml` file components in a common folder at the solution level, for simplicity.

The Cron binding adopts the following configuration:

```
apiVersion: dapr.io/v1alpha1
kind: Component
metadata:
  name: cron
  namespace: default
spec:
  type: bindings.cron
```

```
    metadata:
    - name: schedule
      value: "@every 10s"
```

More information can be found in the Dapr documentation for bindings at `https://docs.dapr.io/developing-applications/building-blocks/bindings/bindings-overview`.

The relevant settings for the configuration of this component of type `bindings.cron` are `name` and `schedule`. With an input binding, the configured name will be used by the Dapr runtime to invoke, as `POST`, the corresponding route at the application endpoint, with the frequency defined in the schedule.

In other input bindings, the trigger will correspond to the arrival of a message or event. Now, we test the binding.

Testing the Cron binding

From an ASP.NET perspective, we need to implement a method with the `cron` route in the ASP.NET controller; this is an example of an addition to the `shipping-service` Dapr project:

```
[HttpPost("cron")]
        public async Task<IActionResult> Cron()
        {
            Console.WriteLine($"Cron @{DateTime.Now.ToString()}
            ");

            return new OkResult();
        }
```

As shown in the preceding code snippet, I am not considering the request payload: the intent with the Cron input binding is just to schedule a recurring request.

By returning a successful result, the ASP.NET controller informs the Dapr runtime that the operation has been completed. It could not be simpler than this.

In the next section, we will learn how to configure and use a more sophisticated output binding.

Using Twilio output bindings in Dapr

An output binding enables our microservice to actively interact with an external system, or service, without having to deal with SDKs, libraries, or APIs other than the Dapr API. In our C# sample, we will use the Dapr .NET SDK to abstract this interaction.

In the previous chapter, *Chapter 5, Publish and Subscribe,* we introduced the Shipping service: this Dapr application subscribes to the `OnOrder_Prepared` topic to be informed once all the steps in the order preparation saga reach a positive conclusion.

We intend to increase the functionality of this microservice by informing the customer that the order shipped. To do so, we can leverage a notification service such as **Twilio** to send the customer a **short message service (SMS)**:

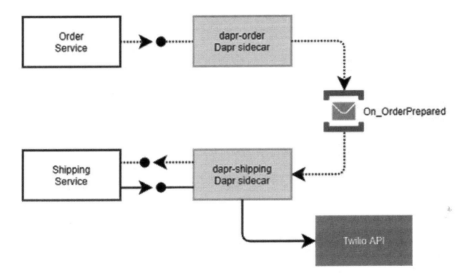

Figure 6.1 – Twilio output binding added to the Shipping service

In *Figure. 6.1*, you can see the evolution of the `shipping-service` Dapr service: an output resource binding of the Twilio type is being adopted.

We will start working on the binding with the next four simple steps:

1. Sign up for a Twilio trial.
2. Configure a Twilio output binding.
3. Signal via the output binding.
4. Verify the notification.

We will begin with the first step and sign up for a Twilio trial.

Signing up for a Twilio trial

The first step is to sign up for a Twilio trial. You can request a Twilio free trial at `https://www.twilio.com/`. As in our sample we are going to send a text message to the customer, you will need to register a valid phone number: I registered my own mobile number for the purpose.

> **Important note**
>
> Be aware of the Twilio limitations for a free trial, which you can find here: `https://support.twilio.com/hc/en-us/articles/360036052753-Twilio-Free-Trial-Limitations`. As an example, you can send text messages only to a validated phone number and the message will start with some default text.

Once you have an account and an active project, there are two strings you need to collect from the Twilio page:

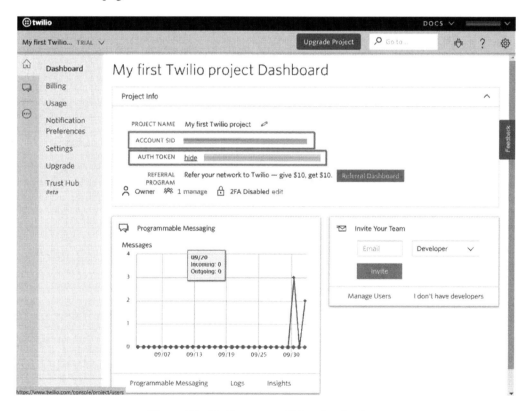

Figure 6.2 – Twilio account SID and auth token

The **ACCOUNT SID** and **AUTH TOKEN** from *Figure 6.2* are the configuration strings that will be used to configure the Twilio binding in Dapr.

Configuring a Twilio output binding

The Twilio binding specification details are available in the Dapr documentation repository at `https://docs.dapr.io/operations/components/setup-bindings/supported-bindings/twilio/`: we have to create a configuration file to access Twilio with our account and credentials. The following is the content of the `components\twilio.yaml` file:

```
apiVersion: dapr.io/v1alpha1
kind: Component
metadata:
  name: twilio
spec:
  type: bindings.twilio.sms
  metadata:
  - name: fromNumber # required.
    value: <omitted>
  - name: accountSid # required.
    value: <omitted>
  - name: authToken # required.
    value: <omitted>
```

Examining the previous configuration file, in the output binding of type `bindings.twilio.sms`, I did not specify the `toNumber` metadata key: this will be influenced by our code.

The `accountSID` and `authToken` keys must be set to the values we gathered from the Twilio web portal.

Next, we will let the application know when a text message should be sent.

Signaling via the output binding

We have to launch our Dapr application and trigger the subscription with a test message.

We can use the Dapr CLI to launch `shipping-service`:

```
dapr run --app-id "shipping-service" --app-port "5005" --dapr-
grpc-port "50050" --dapr-http-port "5050" --components-
path "./components" -- dotnet run --project ./sample.
microservice.shipping/sample.microservice.shipping.csproj
--urls="http://+:5005"
```

In the Dapr output logs, we should see an acknowledgment of the binding sent by the runtime:

```
== DAPR == time="2020-10-03T10:45:38.5706324+02:00" level=info
msg="found component twilio (bindings.twilio.sms)" app_id
=shipping-service instance=DB-SURFACEBOOK2 scope=dapr.runtime
type=log ver=0.10.0
```

The previous Dapr log trace should be followed by a similar output:

```
== DAPR == time="2020-10-03T10:45:44.0528111+02:00" level=info
msg="successful init for output binding twilio (bindings.
twilio.sms)" app_id=shipping-service instance=DB-SURFACEBOOK2
scope=dapr.runtime type=log ver=0.10.0
```

Let's explore how we can use the output binding in our C# code:

```
[Topic(PubSub, Topics.OrderPreparedTopicName)]
[HttpPost(Topics.OrderPreparedTopicName)]
public async Task<ActionResult<Guid>> ship(Shipment
orderShipment, [FromServices] DaprClient daprClient)
{
    var state = await daprClient.
    GetStateEntryAsync<ShippingState>(StoreName,
    orderShipment.OrderId.ToString());
    state.Value ??= new ShippingState() {OrderId =
    orderShipment.OrderId, ShipmentId = Guid.NewGuid()
    };

    await state.SaveAsync();

    // return shipment Id
    var result = state.Value.ShipmentId;
```

```
        Console.WriteLine($"Shipment of orderId
        {orderShipment.OrderId} completed with id
        {result}");

        var metadata = new Dictionary<string,string>();
        metadata.Add("toNumber","<omitted>");
        await daprClient.
        InvokeBindingAsync<string>("twilio","create",
        $"Dear customer, your order with {orderShipment.
        OrderId} completed and shipped", metadata);

        Console.WriteLine($"Shipment of orderId
        {orderShipment.OrderId} notified to customer");

        return result;
    }
```

The instance of `DaprClient` we run in the ASP.NET controller gives us access to the `daprClient.InvokeBindingAsync` method. The `metadata` parameter is a key value dictionary that can be used to influence the metadata configured in `component.yaml`: if you remember, we did not specify the `toNumber` key as it is the microservice's responsibility to gather it from the order (or from another microservice managing the customer data).

The first and second parameters specify the `twilio` name of the configured binding and the intended `create` operation, among those supported by the binding.

We can simulate a message via the Dapr CLI with the `dapr publish` command:

```
dapr publish --pubsub commonpubsub -t OnOrder_Prepared -d
'"{\"OrderId\": \"08ec11cc-7591-4702-bb4d-7e86787b64fe\"}"'
```

From the `shipping-service` output, we see the message has been received and the *shipping* has completed.

All went fine with our code, as the Dapr runtime responded positively to our request. We just need to notify the customer of this as the last step.

Verifying the notification

The Dapr output binding allows us to interact with an external system. Aside from positive feedback (no exceptions) from the Dapr API, there is only one other thing we can do to verify the process completion: check our phone for text messages!

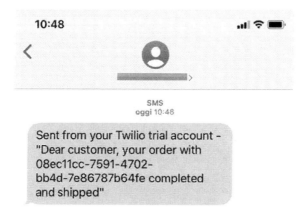

Figure 6.3 – Twilio SMS received

As you see from *Figure 6.3*, we received the notification sent from `shipping-service` via Twilio

In this sample, we triggered a Dapr application via pub/sub, which in turn signaled an event via the output binding. We could also leverage the runtime endpoint to test it directly:

```
POST http://localhost:5050/v1.0/bindings/twilio HTTP/1.1
content-type: application/json

{
    "data": "cookies ready from Dapr",
    "metadata": {
        "toNumber": "<omitted>"
    },
    "operation": "create"
}
```

Consistently with the previous use of the .NET SDK, `toNumber` is set as a value in metadata and `operation` is set to `create`.

We have completed our first sample with the Dapr output binding. In the next section, we will learn how to use the Dapr binding to trigger our microservices.

Ingesting data in C# with the Azure Event Hubs input binding

In a previous section of the chapter, we learned how to implement a simple input binding thanks to the Cron sample. In this section, we will explore another input binding, leveraging the Azure Event Hubs cloud messaging service, by implementing it in the context of `reservation-service`.

The responsibility of `reservation-service` is to allocate quantities of a certain product (cookies) as a new order comes in. In this context, we never considered that if there is a process to reserve (therefore subtracting) quantities, then there should be an equivalent but opposite process to increment the available quantity. This is our chance to fix the business logic of our sample.

In the context of our sample's cookie-selling e-commerce site, let's suppose there is an external service overseeing the manufacturing process, which produces cookies to be sold and/or customized according to customers' requests, depending on forecasts and short-term incoming orders. This manufacturing service is not going to participate with other microservices via Dapr: the only link between the two subsystems is via a stream of events through an Azure Event Hubs channel:

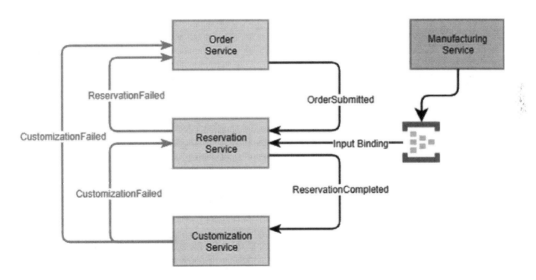

Figure 6.4 – Manufacturing service interaction with Reservation

As seen in *Figure 6.4*, the overall context of the saga, influencing the communication pattern for the requests and compensating the transactions, will be affected by additional data coming from an external subsystem, via a Dapr **Input Binding**, making it all the more important to orchestrate messaging.

This is what we will implement in the following sections.

Creating an Azure Event Hubs binding

In order to configure an Azure Event Hubs input binding, we first have to provision it in Azure.

First, we create an Azure Event Hubs and an event hub. The detailed step-by-step instructions on how to provision these resources on Azure can be found at `https://docs.microsoft.com/en-us/azure/event-hubs/event-hubs-create`.

The following screenshot from the Azure portal shows the result:

Figure 6.5 – Azure Event Hubs policy

As you can see in *Figure 6.5*, I created an Azure Event Hubs **daprbindingehdb** namespace and a **reservationrefill** event hub, and I configured an access policy with listen claims.

The access policy with **Listen** rights should be enough for an input binding: it would have needed the **Send** rights to be used with an output binding instead.

Finally, we need to create an Azure storage account: this resource will be used by the Dapr input binding implementation for Event Hubs to keep track of the offset, the point reached in reading events. Please refer to the step-by-step instructions at `https://docs.microsoft.com/en-us/azure/storage/common/storage-account-create?tabs=azure-portal`.

In the following screenshot, you can see a storage account has been created from the portal:

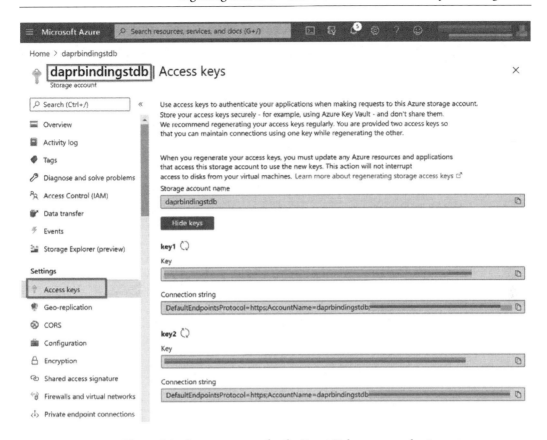

Figure 6.6 – Storage account for the Event Hubs processor host

In *Figure 6.6*, you can see that I created an Azure storage account and obtained the connection string.

This information will be used in the next steps to configure the Dapr component.

Configuring the input binding

Considering the resources that we previously created, the following file in `components\binding-eh.yaml` is needed to instruct Dapr to activate an input binding:

```
apiVersion: dapr.io/v1alpha1
kind: Component
metadata:
  name: reservationinput
  namespace: default
spec:
  type: bindings.azure.eventhubs
```

```yaml
metadata:
- name: connectionString        # Azure EventHubs connection
                                  string
  value: "<omitted>"
- name: consumerGroup           # EventHubs consumer group
  value: "group1"
- name: storageAccountName      # Azure Storage Account Name
  value: "<omitted>"
- name: storageAccountKey       # Azure Storage Account Key
  value: "<omitted>"
- name: storageContainerName    # Azure Storage Container Name
  value: "inputbinding"
```

The Azure Event Hubs specification as a binding is available at `https://docs.dapr.io/operations/components/setup-bindings/supported-bindings/eventhubs/`.

As you can note from the preceding configuration, an Azure storage account is also required to persist Event Hubs checkpoint data.

Dapr is now ready to receive messages (events, in this case). Let's focus on the input binding.

Implementing an Azure Event Hubs input binding

In `reservation-service`, we implement a new method to receive events via the input binding.

As we learned in previous sections, the name of the ASP.NET route must match the name configured in the Dapr component. In the following code snippet, you can see that the attribute reflects the same `reservationinput` component name:

```csharp
[HttpPost("reservationinput")]
        public async Task<IActionResult> Refill([FromServices]
        DaprClient daprClient)
        {
            using (var reader = new System.
            IO.StreamReader(Request.Body))
            {
                var body = await reader.ReadToEndAsync();
                var item = JsonSerializer.
                Deserialize<dynamic>(body);
                var SKU = item.GetProperty("SKU").GetString();
                var Quantity = item.GetProperty("Quantity").
                GetInt32();
```

```
            var stateItem = await daprClient.
            GetStateEntryAsync<ItemState>(StoreName_item,
            SKU);
            stateItem.Value ??= new ItemState() { SKU =
            SKU, Changes = new List<ItemReservation>() };

            stateItem.Value.BalanceQuantity += Quantity;

            await stateItem.SaveAsync();

            Console.WriteLine($"Refill of {SKU}
            for quantity {Quantity}, new balance
            {stateItem.Value.BalanceQuantity}");
        }

        return new OkResult();
    }
```

The method signature we use in this case is slightly different from in the previous sample: we need to interact with the Dapr infrastructure to gather our microservice state; therefore, `daprClient` is now a parameter.

In the preceding code, we are making many assumptions, such as the payload of the messages being JSON and with a specific schema, to keep this exercise simple.

Specific to Dapr, as the event we receive is intended to contain information for a single item, we retrieve the state via the .NET SDK, update the balance quantity, and subsequently save it back to the state store.

Our Dapr `reservation-service` application is ready to receive and process events.

Producing events

Using the Azure Event Hubs documentation (`https://github.com/Azure/azure-sdk-for-net/blob/master/sdk/eventhub/Azure.Messaging.EventHubs/README.md#publish-events-to-an-event-hub`) as a starting point, we can create a C# console project to simulate the output of the Manufacturing service: a continuous stream of new cookies coming out of the ovens is signaled via Azure Event Hubs to the Dapr input binding, as you can see in the following code snippet:

```
class Program
{
    private const string connectionString = "<omitted>";
```

```csharp
    private const string eventHubName = "<omitted>";

static async Task Main(string[] args)
{
    Console.WriteLine("Started sender");

    var rnd = new System.Random();
    var cookies = new List<string>{"bussola1", "bussola8",
    "rockiecookie", "crazycookie", "cookie43"};

    await using (var producerClient = new
    EventHubProducerClient(connectionString, eventHubName))
    {
        do
        {
            using EventDataBatch eventBatch = await
            producerClient.CreateBatchAsync();

            for (int i = 0; i < 3; i++)
            {
                var item = new
                {
                    SKU = cookies[rnd.Next(cookies.Count)],
                    Quantity = 1
                };

                var message = JsonSerializer.
                Serialize(item);
                eventBatch.TryAdd(new EventData(Encoding.
                UTF8.GetBytes(message)));
            }

            await producerClient.SendAsync(eventBatch);

            System.Threading.Thread.Sleep(rnd.
            Next(500,5000));
        } while (true);
    }
}
}
```

The preceding simple code continuously sends a refill of a random selection of a cookie's **stock-keeping unit (SKU)** via Event Hubs to `reservation-service`.

> **Important note**
>
> While working with Azure messaging services such as Azure Service Bus and
> Event Hubs, it is highly recommended to install the Azure Service Bus Explorer
> suite by Paolo Salvatori: you can find out more at `https://github.com/`
> `paolosalvatori/ServiceBusExplorer`.
>
> Although some of the features offered by this powerful tool have been included
> in the Azure portal, the Service Bus Explorer continues to be the best tool for
> anyone developing with the Azure messaging stack.

From the `reservation-service` output, we can verify that the input binding is
receiving events via Dapr from an external subsystem:

```
== APP == Refill of crazycookie for quantity 1, new balance 44
== APP == Refill of bussola1 for quantity 1, new balance 160
== APP == Refill of rockiecookie for quantity 1, new balance
129
== APP == Refill of bussola1 for quantity 1, new balance 161
```

This step concludes the implementation of the input binding in our microservice.

Summary

In this chapter, we focused on the resource binding building blocks of Dapr. Here, we
came to understand how our microservices can react to external events with the Azure
Event Hub input binding. We also learned how, with the Twilio output binding, we can
notify customers via text message without having to deal with libraries, SDKs, and the
plumbing code, as it all boils down to a simple call to the Dapr runtime.

In both input and output bindings samples, a microservice of our e-commerce
architecture is unaware of the implementation details of Twilio and how to interact with
Azure Event Hubs as the messaging bus.

As our sample architecture evolves, we notice the reservation-service microservice sits at
the center of our sample architecture. It is worth noting that the sample code doesn't deal
with application-level retries, which could be relevant if the strong consistency of state
management and an elevated request rate prevent the reservation from always completing
nicely. While this condition should be addressed with more solid code, it does help to
expose a case of potential stress in the application, which you might want to tackle as a
side exercise.

In the next chapter, we will discover how we can tackle this scenario of high-frequency
access to several small, independent state and logic units by introducing Dapr actors.

7
Using Actors

In this chapter, you will learn about the powerful virtual actor model, as implemented in Dapr, and how to leverage it in a microservices-styled architecture, along with the pros and cons of different approaches. The actor model enables your Dapr application to efficiently respond to scenarios of high resource contention, by streamlining the state management. These are the main topics we will discuss in the chapter:

- Using Actors in Dapr
- Actor lifetime, concurrency, and consistency
- Implementing actors in an e-commerce reservation system

The entry barrier for adoption of Actors in Dapr is lower than the complexity behind the core concept of the actor pattern theory. Nonetheless, a solid understanding of the scenarios for Actors—including the ability to recognize bad practices and to avoid any pitfalls—is a prerequisite for their adoption. Therefore, we start with an overview of the actor model before moving on to its lab implementation with Dapr.

Technical requirements

The code for this sample can be found on GitHub at `https://github.com/PacktPublishing/Practical-Microservices-with-Dapr-and-.NET/tree/main/chapter07`.

In this chapter, the working area for the scripts and code is expected to be found at `<repository path>\chapter07\`. In my local environment, it can be found at `C:\Repos\dapr-samples\chapter07`.

Please refer to the *Setting up Dapr* section in *Chapter 1, Introducing Dapr*, for a complete guide on the tools needed to develop with Dapr and work with the samples.

Using Actors in Dapr

The actor model in Dapr adopts the concept of **virtual actors**: a simplified approach to a complex combination of design challenges. Virtual actors originate from the Microsoft "Orleans" project, a project that inspired the design of Dapr; in case you want to deepen your knowledge of its history, the research paper can be found at `https://www.microsoft.com/en-us/research/project/orleans-virtual-actors/`.

In the virtual actor pattern, the state and behavior of a service are tightly intertwined, and the actor's lifetime gets orchestrated by an external service, or runtime. The developers are lifted from the responsibility of governing concurrent access to the resource (the virtual actor) and to its underlying state.

These concepts will become clearer by analyzing how the virtual actor pattern is implemented in Dapr, as presented in the next section.

Introduction to the actor pattern

In Dapr, the interaction between a client and a service counterpart happens via a direct call, with a service-to-service invocation, or indirectly via a message, with *publish* and *subscribe*, as seen in the previous chapters. The Dapr application acting as the service then accesses the state to read and/or manipulate it.

If we consider the components involved in this class of interactions, it all boils down to the following:

- A client remote call

- A service processing the request

- A database managing the stored information

We have just listed the same number of interactions in a classic three-tier architecture. A microservice architecture affects several aspects of client/service communication by introducing new patterns and capabilities; nevertheless, it can't escape the laws of physics, such as network latency and storage **input/output (I/O)** latency.

As our Dapr application is going to operate in a highly distributed environment (starting from *Chapter 8*, *Deployment to Kubernetes*), the three aforementioned components could possibly be located in separate nodes or even be part of different services, and therefore traverse network and/or application boundaries, each of which adds its share of latency.

Caching helps to reduce latency, bringing information closer to the service, by improving the performance of repeated reads from the source of information: the database. At the same time, it introduces the complexity of managing consistency, previously solved by the database: it's difficult to keep a cache relevant while updates are performed. Once you try to solve the consistency issue by controlling the access to cached information, the complexity of concurrency promptly emerges.

Caching is a powerful mechanism but, once you try to strengthen it from its consistency and concurrency perspectives, it risks falling short of its declared objective. The virtual actor pattern implemented in Dapr tries to approach this quest differently.

It could help our understanding of the actor model if we consider the starting point and its challenges. Let's do this by analyzing the current status of the backend of our cookie-selling *Biscotti Brutti Ma Buoni* e-commerce site.

The following screenshot depicts the interactions between our sample's Dapr applications and their state:

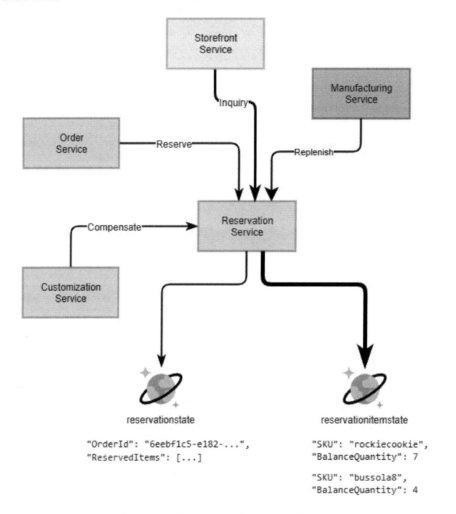

Figure 7.1 – Status quo of sample architecture

As you can see in *Figure 7.1*, the **Reservation Service** (also known as the `reservation-service` Dapr application) sits at the center of many interactions, participating with other Dapr applications in the saga we explored in *Chapter 5, Publish and Subscribe*, receiving updates from the manufacturing service, and responding to requests from our storefront service (which is generic, as a much richer **user interface** (**UI**) is out of this book's scope).

The Dapr application relies on two state stores, detailed as follows:

- The `reservationstate` state store keeps track of the products (SKU) reserved by an order, useful when compensating the order in the case of a product customization failure.

  We can predict there will be a limited number of interactions with the state for the specific order of successfully fulfilled ones.

  The population of `reservationstate` is always increasing, with operations concentrated on the state for newly added orders.

- The `reservationitemstate` state store is used differently: it keeps track of the balance of each product's quantity; orders diminish its value, while replenishments increase it. Each order (and the potential compensating activities), storefront request, or manufacturing action equates to a state retrieval and update for the specific item.

  We adopt strong concurrency in managing the `reservation-service` state, to avoid inconsistent updates: as a side effect, we risk increasing conflicts of updates in the case of a sustained growth in requests, leading to more retries to avoid transferring the impact onto clients.

  The population of `reservationitemstate` is stable over time, one for each SKU, with operations being distributed evenly or unevenly depending on the SKU's popularity.

As you can notice from *Figure 7.1*, the very same amount of data retrieval or manipulation requests is reaching the state store—the Azure Cosmos DB in our sample.

By introducing the Dapr actor model, we can create a virtual representation of each `reservationitemstate` state and bind it together with the service code counterpart.

The following screenshot shows where the Dapr actor model will be introduced:

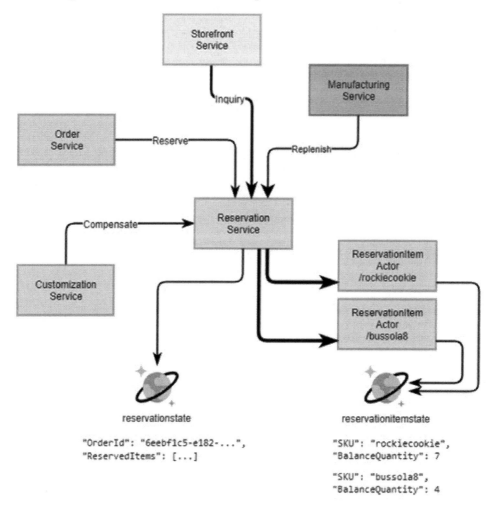

Figure 7.2 – Dapr actor model introduced in sample architecture

Figure 7.2 shows an evolution of our sample architecture: we introduce a new `reservationactor-service` Dapr service, which offers access to the population of Dapr Actors of type `ReservationItemActor`.

As we will learn later in this chapter, Dapr manages the lifetime and distribution of actors in the hosting environment (locally or in Kubernetes): we can expect that each of the SKUs typically sold by our e-commerce site will have a corresponding actor instance ready to receive requests.

What do Dapr (virtual) Actors provide to our sample microservice architecture? The business logic that manages the SKU balance quantity, refactored from `reservation-service` to the code of the `ReservationItemActor` actor, will leverage the state now being maintained in the actor instance itself, kept closely in sync by the Dapr runtime.

With Actors in Dapr, the state and the behavior become intertwined, and load gets distributed over the hosting platform for resiliency: no additional effort is required to the developer, as all aspects are managed by the Dapr runtime and platform.

Access to a Dapr actor is governed by a turn-based policy: a read operation will find the state information in memory, equally as fast as an item in cache, while update operations will reach the state store's database without facing the concurrency issues we have discussed so far.

Before we finish this overview, let's see how we can configure a state store for Actors in Dapr.

Configuring the new state store

We learned how to configure a state store in *Chapter 4, Introducing State Management*, from which we remember that only a few of the currently available state stores in Dapr can be used with actors: the Azure Cosmos DB state store is one of these.

The following, `yaml` file is an example of a state store configuration:

```yaml
apiVersion: dapr.io/v1alpha1
kind: Component
metadata:
  name: reservationitemactorstore
  namespace: default
spec:
  type: state.azure.cosmosdb
  metadata:
  - name: url
    value: ...omitted...
  - name: masterKey
    value: ...omitted...
  - name: database
    value: state
  - name: collection
    value: reservationitemactorstore
  - name: actorStateStore
    value: "true"
```

The changes to support the actor model are minimal: we only need to set the `actorStateStore` metadata to `true`.

Now that we have configured a new state store, which I named `reservationitemactorstore`, we should verify it.

Verifying the configuration

We can verify that the configuration has been applied by launching any of the existing Dapr applications: it will look for the `yaml` files in the `components` path.

From the following Dapr application log, only the significant lines have been extracted:

```
== DAPR == time="2020-10-14T19:38:22.3297439+02:00"
level=warning msg="either no actor state store or multiple
actor state stores are specified in the configuration, actor
stores specified: 0" app_id=order-service instance=DB-
SURFACEBOOK2 scope=dapr.runtime type=log ver=0.11.2

== DAPR == time="2020-10-14T19:38:22.3297439+02:00" level=info
msg="component loaded. name: customizationstore, type: state.
azure.cosmosdb" app_id=order-service instance=DB-SURFACEBOOK2
scope=dapr.runtime type=log ver=0.11.2
```

In the previous output, we can see the message `"either no actor state store or multiple actor state stores are specified"` is presented when a state store is found that is not configured as an actor state store:

```
== DAPR == time="2020-10-14T19:38:22.8820627+02:00" level=info
msg="component loaded. name: reservationitemactorstore, type:
state.azure.cosmosdb" app_id=order-service instance=DB-
SURFACEBOOK2 scope=dapr.runtime type=log ver=0.11.2

== DAPR == time="2020-10-14T19:38:23.5358829+02:00" level=info
msg="actor runtime started. actor idle timeout: 1h0m0s.
actor scan interval: 30s" app_id=order-service instance=DB-
SURFACEBOOK2 scope=dapr.runtime.actor type=log ver=0.11.2

== DAPR == time="2020-10-14T19:38:23.5358829+02:00" level=info
msg="starting connection attempt to placement service: lo
calhost:6050" app_id=order-service instance=DB-SURFACEBOOK2
scope=dapr.runtime.actor type=log ver=0.11.2
...
== DAPR == time="2020-10-14T19:38:23.5628868+02:00" level=info
msg="established connection to placement service at local
host:6050" app_id=order-service instance=DB-SURFACEBOOK2
scope=dapr.runtime.actor type=log ver=0.11.2
```

As it has not been preceded by any warning message, the `reservationitemactorstore` component has been recognized as a state store for actors. If you wrongfully configured two state stores as `actorStateStore` you would receive the same warning we saw before, as only one is permitted: no warning is a good sign. In the last output message, we have confirmation the connection to the Dapr placement service has been established.

This extensive overview gave us a better understanding of how Actors in Dapr work to help us build scalable applications. Before we move on to the implementation, we need to understand a few more concepts, including the actor's lifetime.

Actor lifetime, concurrency, and consistency

The Dapr actor model relies on two main components: the Dapr runtime, operating in the sidecar, and the Dapr Placement service.

Placement service

The Placement service has the responsibility of keeping a map of the Dapr instances capable of serving actors: considering our sample, the `reservationactor-service` application is an example of such a service.

Once a new instance of our new `reservationactor-service` Dapr application starts, it informs the Placement service that it is ready to serve actors of the `ReservationItemActor` type.

The Placement service broadcasts a map—in the form of a hash table with the hosts' information and the served actor types—to all of the Dapr sidecars operating in the environment.

Thanks to this constant update of the hosts' map, actors are uniformly distributed over the actor service instances.

In the Kubernetes deployment mode of Dapr, the host is a **pod** (a group of containers that are deployed together), while in the standalone mode the host is the local node itself. In Kubernetes, pods can be terminated or initiated in response to many events (such as a scaleout of pods and nodes, or a node being evicted from the cluster to be upgraded, added, or removed).

Considering our sample that is deployed in a Kubernetes cluster, we expect to have at least three replicated pods with `reservationactor-service` running together with the Dapr sidecar container. If our cookie-selling e-commerce site has about 300 active cookies' SKUs, approximately 100 actors of type `ReservationItemActor` would reside in each of the `reservationactor-service` pods.

You can learn more about the Placement service in the Dapr documentation at `https://docs.dapr.io/developing-applications/building-blocks/actors/actors-background/#actor-placement-service`.

We can now move forward to learn how the Dapr actor model deals with concurrency and consistency.

Concurrency and consistency

The actor model's implementation in Dapr approaches the state's concurrency manipulation by enforcing a turn-based access with per-actor locks. The lock is acquired at the beginning of each interaction and is released afterward.

The following screenshot shows the turn-based access on Dapr actors:

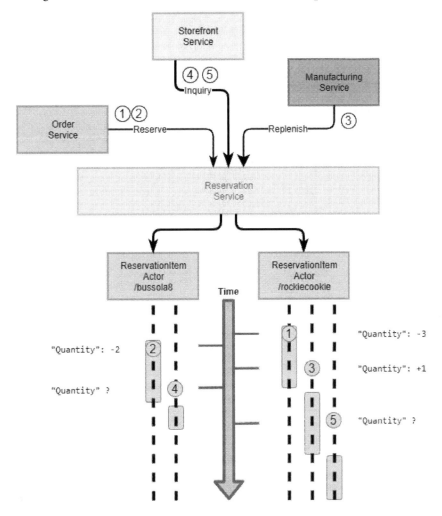

Figure 7.3 – Turn-based concurrency access to Dapr actors

In *Figure 7.3*, we can appreciate the impact of locks being acquired and released on a per-actor basis. Considering the two actors in the example— the `ReservationItemActor` actor for the **bussola8** SKU and the `ReservationItemActor` actor for the **rockiecookie** SKU—these steps correspond to client (other Dapr or non-Dapr applications) requests in order of time, as follows:

1. A request to reserve a quantity on the actor with ID **rockiecookie**: the actor is ready and no locks are present, therefore it is immediately granted and the interaction can start immediately.

2. A request to reserve a quantity on the actor with ID **bussola8**: this actor is ready with no locks present either, so the interaction can start immediately.

3. A request to replenish the quantity for actor ID **rockiecookie** is received: the actor is locked since *step 1* has not completed yet, therefore the request waits for the lock to be released. Once the actor becomes available, the interaction can start.

4. A request to retrieve the current balance quantity for actor ID **bussola8** is received: the actor is still locked with *step 2*, therefore the request waits for it to be released. Once the actor becomes available, the quick (read) operation can happen.

5. A similar request reaches the actor ID **rockiecookie**: as all interactions with the actor are treated equally and the actor is locked working on *step 3*, the request waits for the lock's release to quickly interact with the actor.

None of these interactions required any additional effort from the Dapr applications' code: everything is handled by the Dapr runtime.

While turn-based access to Dapr Actors imposes a strict concurrency control, it's important to remember it is enforced on a per-actor basis: concurrent requests to different actors can be fulfilled independently at the same time.

This approach gives Dapr an advantage in maintaining data consistency while acting as a cache at the same time: as the actor's state could be as simple as a record in the Dapr state store, receiving data manipulation requests on a specific record with a serial approach puts any database in the best conditions to operate.

From the individual actor's perspective, it's important to avoid executing long or variable operations as these would influence the lock duration and impact client interaction. As an example, an actor should avoid I/O operations, or any other blocking interaction.

The actor pattern is best used with many fast, independent actors. From a client perspective, though, trying to coordinate or aggregate information from too many actors might not result in the best possible experience. As we learned in *Chapter 4, Introducing State Management*, it's possible to submit queries directly to the underlying database to extract or aggregate data from state stores.

In our specific sample, the `reservation-service` evolves from being the Dapr application in charge of managing the `reservationitemstate` state, to become the main client of the `ReservationItemActor` actor type, part of the `reservationactor-service` application.

Any Dapr-enabled application has the ability to interact with the Actors, via a **software development kit (SDK)** or by directly invoking the Dapr **application programming interface (API)** at the endpoint exposed by the Dapr sidecar.

At this stage in the development of Actors in Dapr, an actor cannot directly subscribe to a publish/subscribe topic: this is an example in which an Actor needs to be invoked indirectly from another service.

There is still one major concept left to assimilate on the Dapr actor model: the actor's lifetime.

Lifetime

Actors in Dapr are not explicitly created: they are brought to life by invoking them (say Actor, Actor, Actor three times in front of a mirror and they will appear!) instead. In the scope of the Dapr .NET SDK, the actor implementation can override the `OnActivateAsync` method from the base class to intercept the activation moment.

An actor will be deactivated after a period of inactivity. Deactivation is temporary, as the Dapr runtime is ready to rehydrate it back into memory from the persisted state store if a new request arises. The idle timeout of each actor type can be configured, so in your architecture you can define both long-running actors and short-lived ones. An actor instance can become aware of its deactivation by overriding the `OnDeactivateAsync` method of the base class. Any interaction with the actor's instance extends its lifetime, by restarting the timeout clock.

Reminders and Timers are two important features of Dapr Actors. Both are useful to schedule an activity on an actor, whether it is recurring or intended to be executed only once: as an example, you want to delay the execution of your service code from the initial request. The two differ in behavior, as highlighted here:

- Timers can trigger while the actor is active, but once deactivated the Timer is no longer effective and it does not keep the actor active.

- Reminders are persistent, as they trigger the registered method even on a deactivated actor. As a consequence, a Reminder extends the actor's lifetime.

Now we have learned about the lifetime, placement, consistency, and concurrency of the Dapr actor model, we are ready to apply this knowledge and implement the changes discussed so far in our small e-commerce solution.

Implementing actors in an e-commerce reservation system

Equipped with the information on the Actor's pattern and with a plan to implement an evolution of our sample project by introducing Dapr actors, we now have several steps to complete, listed as follows:

1. Create the Actor's projects.

2. Implement the actor's model.

3. Access actors from other Dapr applications.

4. Inspect the Actor's state.

Let's start by creating the .NET projects.

Preparing the Actor's projects

To implement actors with Dapr in C#, we have to create an actor interface project separate from the actor's service implementation in two projects.

The actor's interface will be referenced by the other services or clients that need to interact with the actors. Here, we create the interface project, as follows:

```
PS C:\Repos\dapr-samples\chapter07> dotnet new classlib -f
netcoreapp3.1 -o sample.microservice.reservationitemactor.
interfaces
PS C:\Repos\dapr-samples\chapter07> cd .\sample.microservice.
```

```
reservationactor.interfaces\
PS C:\Repos\dapr-samples\chapter07\sample.microservice.
reservationactor.service> dotnet add package Dapr.Actors -v
0.11.0-preview01
```

The following command is going to be the project for the `reservationactor-service` Dapr application:

```
PS C:\Repos\dapr-samples\chapter07> dotnet new webapi -f
netcoreapp3.1 -o sample.microservice.reservationitemactor.
service
PS C:\Repos\dapr-samples\chapter07> cd .\sample.microservice.
reservationactor.service\
PS C:\Repos\dapr-samples\chapter07\sample.microservice.
reservationactor.service> dotnet add reference ..\sample.
microservice.reservationactor.interfaces\sample.microservice.
reservationactor.interfaces.csproj
PS C:\Repos\dapr-samples\chapter07\sample.microservice.
reservationactor.service> dotnet add package Dapr.Actors -v
0.11.0-preview01
PS C:\Repos\dapr-samples\chapter07\sample.microservice.
reservationactor.service> dotnet add package Dapr.Actors.
AspNetCore -v 0.11.0-preview01
```

Each project also refers to the .NET SDK for Actors, located in the `Dapr.Actors` package, and the `reservationactor-service` project refers to the `Dapr.Actors.AspNetCore` package for Actors in ASP.NET Core.

Our projects are ready, so we can proceed to implement the Actors.

Implementing the actor's model

We start by implementing the actor interface in the `IReservationItemActor.cs` class of the `sample.microservice.reservationitemactor.interfaces` project, as follows:

```
using Dapr.Actors;
using System.Threading.Tasks;

namespace sample.microservice.reservationactor.interfaces
{
    public interface IReservationItemActor : IActor
    {
```

```
        Task<int> AddReservation(int quantity);
        Task<int> GetBalance();
        Task RegisterReminder();
        Task UnregisterReminder();
        Task RegisterTimer();
        Task UnregisterTimer();
    }
}
```

The `IReservationItemActor` interface, inheriting from `IActor` in `Dapr.Actors`, is as simple as the tasks our actor will fulfill: `AddReservation` to receive a reservation for a SKU, and to return its available quantity via `GetBalance`. The other methods are left in the code to show additional features of Dapr Actors and originate from the sample in the Dapr repository at `https://github.com/dapr/dotnet-sdk/blob/master/docs/get-started-dapr-actor.md`.

Let's move on to the implementation in the `ReservationItemActor.cs` class in the `sample.microservice.reservationactor.service.service` project, as follows:

```
using Dapr.Actors;
using Dapr.Actors.Runtime;
using System;
using System.Threading.Tasks;
using sample.microservice.reservationactor.interfaces;
using sample.microservice.state.reservationactor;
using System.Collections.Generic;

namespace sample.microservice.reservationactor.service
{
    internal class ReservationItemActor : Actor,
    IReservationItemActor, IRemindable
    {
        public const string StateName = "reservationitem";

        public ReservationItemActor(ActorService actorService,
        ActorId actorId)
            : base(actorService, actorId)
        {
        }

        protected override Task OnActivateAsync()
        {
            Console.WriteLine($"Activating actor id: {this.
```

```
        Id}");
        return Task.CompletedTask;
    }

    protected override Task OnDeactivateAsync()
    {
        Console.WriteLine($"Deactivating actor id: {this.
          Id}");
        return Task.CompletedTask;
    }
... class continue below ...
```

In the previous section from the `ReservationItemActor.cs` file, we can see a typical definition of a Dapr Actor type in C#: the `ReservationItemActor` class derives from `Dapr.Actors.Runtime.Actor`, and implements the interface of our `IReservationItemActor` Actor interface and the `IRemindable` interface from the `Dapr.Actors.Runtime` namespace. This last interface is used to enable Reminders, a powerful feature to influence the Actor life cycle.

The `ReservationItemActor.cs` file continues here:

```
... class continue from above ...
        public async Task<int> AddReservation(int quantity)
        {
            var SKU = this.Id.GetId();

            var state = await this.StateManager.
            TryGetStateAsync<ItemState>(StateName);

... omitted ...

            await this.StateManager.SetStateAsync<ItemState>(
                StateName, value);
            Console.WriteLine($"Balance of {SKU} was
            {initialBalanceQuantity}, now {value.
            BalanceQuantity}");

            return value.BalanceQuantity;
        }

        public async Task<int> GetBalance()
        {
            var state = await this.StateManager.
            GetStateAsync<ItemState>(StateName);
```

```
                    return state.BalanceQuantity;
            }
  … omitted …
  }
```

In the methods' implementation, it's worth noting how an instance can access the state store via the Dapr Actor object model.

With the `TryGetStateAsync<type>(StateName)` method of `StateManager`, implemented in the `Dapr.Actors.Runtime.Actor` base class, the actor attempts to retrieve a state with a `StateName` key from the store, as it does not exist yet. Alternatively, you can use `StateManager.GetStateAsync<type>(StateName)`.

With the `StateManager.SetStateAsync<type>(StateName, value)` method, you inform the Dapr runtime to save the serializable `value` in state with the `StateName` key after the actor method completes successfully.

Our actor implementation is not ready yet: the actor type we just implemented must be registered with the Dapr runtime. The following is from the `Program.cs` file:

```
using Microsoft.AspNetCore.Builder;
using Microsoft.AspNetCore.Hosting;
using Microsoft.Extensions.Hosting;
using Dapr.Actors.AspNetCore;
using Microsoft.AspNetCore;

namespace sample.microservice.reservationactor.service
{
    public class Program
    {
        public static void Main(string[] args)
        {
            CreateWebHostBuilder(args).Build().Run();
        }

        public static IWebHostBuilder
        CreateWebHostBuilder(string[] args) =>
            WebHost.CreateDefaultBuilder(args)
                .UseStartup<Startup>()
                .UseActors(actorRuntime =>
                {
                    actorRuntime.
                    RegisterActor<ReservationItemActor>();
```

```
                        });
        }
}
```

As you can see, an actor service has a different implementation than a standard service in Dapr, also from a configuration perspective.

The ASP.NET project implementing our Dapr Actors is now ready to be made reachable by the other Dapr applications.

Accessing actors from the other Dapr applications

First, we create a separate project to contain the actor interface so that we can reference it from clients.

As depicted in *Figure 7.2*, we decided to keep the interaction with actors of type `ReservationItemActor` in the scope of `reservationactor-service`. We will add the reference here, as follows:

```
PS C:\Repos\dapr-samples\chapter07> cd .\sample.microservice.
reservation\
PS C:\Repos\dapr-samples\chapter07\sample.microservice.
reservation> dotnet add reference ..\sample.microservice.
reservationactor.interfaces\sample.microservice.
reservationactor.interfaces.csproj
```

We should also add the reference to the `Dapr.Actors` package in `reservationactor-service`, as we did in the previous projects.

In the previous chapters, our code directly accessed the state store information via the `DaprClient` instance our ASP.Net controllers have been injected with by Dapr. The change we apply mostly to `ReservationController.cs` will only impact this:

```
[Topic(PubSub, common.Topics.OrderSubmittedTopicName)]
[HttpPost(common.Topics.OrderSubmittedTopicName)]
public async Task<ActionResult<OrderReservation>>
ReserveOrder(Order order, [FromServices] DaprClient daprClient)
{
        var stateReservation = await daprClient.
        GetStateEntryAsync<ReservationState>(StoreName_
        reservation, order.Id.ToString());
        stateReservation.Value ??= new ReservationState() {
        OrderId = order.Id, ReservedItems = new
```

```
         List<ItemReservation>() };

         var result = new OrderReservation(){ OrderId =
         order.Id, ReservedItems = new List<Item>()};
         foreach (var item in order.Items)
         {
             var SKU = item.ProductCode;
             var quantity = item.Quantity;

             var actorID = new ActorId(SKU);
             var proxy = ActorProxy.
             Create<IReservationItemActor>
             (actorID,"ReservationItemActor");
             var balanceQuantity = await proxy.
             AddReservation(quantity);

             result.ReservedItems.Add(new Item{SKU = SKU,
             BalanceQuantity = balanceQuantity});
}
```

There are a few things to examine in the previous code snippet. By instantiating the `ActorId(SKU)` type we pass as a parameter in `ActorProxy.Create<IReservationItemActor>(actorID, "ReservationItemActor")`, we are instructing the Dapr runtime to look for—in the map kept in sync by the Dapr Placement service—the actor service instance responsible for handling the specific actor with a key equal to the SKU.

The instance of `Dapr.Actors.Client.ActorProxy` we just created lets us invoke the Actor leveraging its interface as if it were a local object. The `proxy.AddReservation(quantity)` method is what we defined previously in the `IReservationItemActor` interface and implemented in `ReservationItemActor`.

All the concepts previously described in this chapter hide behind this simple object model—isn't it nice, elegant, and simple?

We can launch the Dapr applications as before, with the **command-line interface (CLI)** or Tye, now with the addition of the newly created `reservationactor-service` Actor service from the `sample.microservice.reservationactor.service.csproj` project, as follows:

```
dapr run --app-id "reservationactor-service" --app-port "5004"
--dapr-grpc-port "50040" --dapr-http-port "5014" --components-
path "./components" -- dotnet run --project ./sample.
microservice.reservationactor.service/sample.microservice.
```

```
reservationactor.service.csproj --urls="http://+:5004"
```

We can submit an order invoking the ASP.NET controller in `order-service`, currently configured to be exposed at `http://localhost:5001/order`, to appreciate the changes applied to the architecture. The following is the output from `reservation-service`:

```
== APP == Reservation in d6082d80-1239-45db-9d35-95e587d7b299
of rockiecookie for 4, balance 32
== APP == Reservation in d6082d80-1239-45db-9d35-95e587d7b299
of bussola8 for 7, balance 59
== APP == Reservation in d6082d80-1239-45db-9d35-95e587d7b299
of crazycookie for 2, balance 245
== APP == Reservation in d6082d80-1239-45db-9d35-95e587d7b299
completed
```

Let's focus on the output from `reservationactor-service`, shown here:

```
== APP == Actor: rockiecookie Activated
== APP == Balance of rockiecookie was 36, now 32
== APP == Activating actor id: bussola8
== APP == Actor: bussola8 Activated
== APP == Balance of bussola1 was 6, now 4
== APP == Balance of crazycookie was 247, now 245
```

We can see from the output messages that some actors have been implicitly activated by interacting with them, while other ones were already active in the host memory.

Now that we have proved how easy it is to introduce the actor model into an existing Dapr application, we should verify how our actors' data gets persisted.

Inspecting the actor state

We learned to configure a Dapr state store to make it suitable for actors. It is interesting to note how the state key is composed, as you can see from the following item in Azure Cosmos DB, corresponding to an actor state:

```
{
    "id": "reservationactor-service||ReservationItemActor||cook
ie2||reservationitem",
    "value": {
        "BalanceQuantity": -12,
        "Changes": [
            {
```

```
                    "Quantity": 12,
                    "ReservedOn": "2020-10-09T22:17:47.0511873Z",
                    "SKU": "cookie2"
            }
        ],
        "SKU": "cookie2"
    },
    "partitionKey": "reservationactor-service||
    ReservationItemActor||cookie2",
    "_rid": "h+ETAIFd00cBAAAAAAAAAA==",
    "_self": "dbs/h+ETAA==/colls/h+ETAIFd00c=/docs/
    h+ETAIFd00cBAAAAAAAAAA==/",
    "_etag": "\"0000dd23-0000-0d00-0000-5f80e18a0000\"",
    "_attachments": "attachments/",
    "_ts": 1602281866
}
```

As you see, the key is composed with the pattern `<application ID>||<actor type>||<actor Id>||<key>`, where the following applies:

- `reservationactor-service` is the application ID.

- `actor Id` is the actor's **unique identifier** (**UID**) we chose to adopt the SKU—here, `cookie2`.

- `ReservationItemActor` is the actor type.

- `key` identifies the state key used—`reservationitem` here: an actor can have multiple states.

We have completed our journey of learning about the actor model in Dapr.

Summary

In this chapter, we learned that the actor's model supported by Dapr is a very powerful tool in our toolbox.

We understood the scenarios that benefit the most from applying actors, and how to avoid the most common implementation pitfalls.

By configuring Dapr Actors, from the state store to the ASP.NET Core perspective, we appreciated how the simplicity of Dapr extends to this building block too.

We introduced an actor type in our existing architecture: by that, we learned how to separate the contract (interface) from the implementation and invoke it from other Dapr services.

We should also realize this is another example of how Dapr facilitates the development of microservices architectures by addressing the communication and discovery of services (how easy is it for a client to interact with an actor?) and unleashing the independent evolution of our architecture's components, as the introduction of actors in our sample has been seamless for the rest of the services. With this new information and experience, you will be able to identify how to best introduce Dapr Actors in your new or existing solution.

Our sample solution is complete, and we are ready to move it to an environment capable of exposing it to the hungry and festive customers of *Biscotti Brutti Ma Buoni*. Starting from the next chapter, we will learn how to prepare the Dapr-based solution to deploy it on Kubernetes.

Section 3: Deploying and Scaling Dapr Solutions

As you know how Dapr works and have learned how to create applications with Dapr, it is time to deploy to Kubernetes and load test the applications.

This section has the following chapters:

- *Chapter 8, Deploying to Kubernetes*
- *Chapter 9, Tracing Dapr Applications*
- *Chapter 10, Load Testing and Scaling Dapr*

8
Deploying to Kubernetes

In this chapter, we will shift our focus to the Kubernetes hosting mode known as Dapr. First, we will learn how to prepare our sample projects so that they can be deployed in a containerized form, before moving on to preparing Dapr in the Azure Kubernetes Service cluster.

This chapter will help us gain visibility of the production-ready environment for a solution based on Dapr: a Kubernetes cluster.

In this chapter, we will cover the following topics:

- Setting up Kubernetes
- Setting up Dapr on Kubernetes
- Deploying a Dapr application to Kubernetes
- Exposing Dapr applications to external clients

As developers and architects, while we mainly focus on the definition and implementation of a solution. However, it is equally as important to understand the implications of the deployment options and how these can influence our design choices and impact our overall solution architecture.

Our first objective is to provision the Kubernetes cluster and connect to it from our development environment.

Technical requirements

The code for the examples in this chapter can be found in this book's GitHub repository at `https://github.com/PacktPublishing/Practical-Microservices-with-Dapr-and-.NET/tree/main/chapter08`.

In this chapter, the working area for scripts and code is expected to be `<repository path>\chapter08\`. In my local environment, it is `C:\Repos\dapr-samples\chapter08`.

Please refer to the *Setting up Dapr* section in *Chapter 1, Introducing Dapr*, for a complete guide on the tools needed to develop with Dapr and work with the examples in this book.

Setting up Kubernetes

While the discussion around microservice architectures has evolved independently, the concept of containerized deployments has propelled its popularity among developers and architects.

Once you start to have a multitude of microservices, each comprising one or many containers, you soon realize you need a piece of software that deals with the orchestration of these containers. In a nutshell, orchestration is the reason why Kubernetes is so relevant and frequently appears in the context of microservice architectures.

> **Important note**
> **Kubernetes** is the most popular open source container orchestrator and is a project maintained by the **Cloud Native Computing Foundation** (**CNCF**). To learn more about Kubernetes, I suggest that you read straight from the source at `https://kubernetes.io/docs/concepts/overview/what-is-kubernetes/`.

In this section, we are going to provision an **Azure Kubernetes Service** (**AKS**) cluster. Even if it is not in this book's scope to learn all the details of AKS, for those of you who are not already Kubernetes geeks, it will be helpful for you to become familiar with some of the concepts and tooling.

These are the steps we will be going through:

1. Creating an Azure Resource Group

2. Creating an AKS cluster

3. Connecting to the AKS cluster

Let's start by preparing a Resource Group.

Creating an Azure Resource Group

In a Windows terminal, log into Azure by using the Azure CLI. We could also use the portal here, but the CLI helps us keep a consistent experience between Azure and Kubernetes:

```
az login
```

Let's connect to the subscription that we want to provision the cluster in. It will probably be the same Azure subscription you used in the previous chapters. Mine is named Sandbox:

```
az account set --subscription "Sandbox"
```

All the commands that we will be issuing via the Azure CLI will be issued in the context of the specified Azure subscription.

Creating an AKS cluster

Now, we can create the AKS cluster. Please check the walkthrough available at https://docs.microsoft.com/en-us/azure/aks/kubernetes-walkthrough for additional information.

In the following CLI command, we are choosing to enable the monitoring feature and preferring the use of VirtualMachineScaleSets (an Azure feature that lets you manage and scale nodes as a group) for the nodes rather than a simple VM:

```
az aks create --resource-group daprk8srgdb --name daprk8saksdb `
    --node-count 3 --node-vm-size Standard_D2s_v3 `
    --enable-addons monitoring `
    --vm-set-type VirtualMachineScaleSets `
    --generate-ssh-keys
```

After waiting a few minutes for the cluster to be created, we can verify the status of the AKS cluster resource with the following command:

```
az aks show --name daprk8saksdb --resource-group daprk8srgdb
```

Once we have successfully created the AKS cluster, we can connect to it.

Connecting to the AKS cluster

Once the cluster has been created, we need to install the Kubernetes tools on our development environment, namely the **kubectl CLI**, which is facilitated by the Azure CLI, with the following command:

```
az aks install-cli
```

With the Azure CLI, we can also retrieve the credentials we need in order to gain administrative access to the cluster. These credentials will be merged into the default location for the Kubernetes configuration file:

```
az aks get-credentials --name daprk8saksdb --resource-group
daprk8srgdb
Merged "daprk8saksdb" as current context in C:\Users\dabedin\.
kube\config
```

We now have access to the cluster, and with the `kubectl` CLI, we can control any aspect of it. As a starting point, let's examine the cluster's composition:

```
kubectl get nodes
NAME                              STATUS    ROLES    AGE
VERSION
aks-nodepool1-84704866-vmss000003 Ready     agent    11m
v1.17.11
aks-nodepool1-84704866-vmss000004 Ready     agent    11m
v1.17.11
aks-nodepool1-84704866-vmss000005 Ready     agent    11m
v1.17.11
```

According to the `kubectl get nodes` command, we have three nodes running, as specified in the AKS provisioning command.

From this point forward, the experience will have less to do with Azure and more to do with Dapr and Kubernetes. Due to this, it will apply to any suitable similar containerized environment, such as other cloud providers or edge/hybrid scenarios. I suggest getting familiar with the `kubectl` CLI documentation, which is available at `https://kubernetes.io/docs/reference/kubectl/`.

Optionally, you can install the client tools for **Helm** in your development environment. Helm is a package manager for Kubernetes, often used by more complex solutions. To learn more, take a look at the documentation at `https://helm.sh/docs/intro/install/`.

In this section, we managed to create an Azure Kubernetes Service, install the necessary Kubernetes tools locally, and gain access to the cluster itself. The next step is to install Dapr in our AKS cluster.

Setting up Dapr on Kubernetes

At this stage, a Kubernetes cluster – specifically AKS on Azure – is ready to accommodate our workload. We need to install Dapr before we can move on to the preparation phase for our applications.

In *Chapter 1, Introducing Dapr*, we used the following command, which we'll use again here, to initialize Dapr in Kubernetes:

```
PS C:\Repos\dapr-samples\chapter08> dapr init -k
Making the jump to hyperspace...
Note: To install Dapr using Helm, see here:  https://docs.dapr.
io/getting-started/install-dapr/#install-with-helm-advanced
Deploying the Dapr control plane to your cluster...
Success! Dapr has been installed to namespace dapr-system. To
verify, run `dapr status -k' in your terminal. To get started,
go here: https://aka.ms/dapr-getting-started
```

The previous command installs and initializes the Dapr components in the cluster corresponding to the current Kubernetes configuration.

We can verify that the Dapr service we learned about in *Chapter 1, Introducing Dapr*, is now present in the cluster by executing the following command in the Dapr CLI:

```
PS C:\Repos\dapr-samples\chapter08> dapr status -k
  NAME                         NAMESPACE      HEALTHY  STATUS
REPLICAS  VERSION  AGE  CREATED
  dapr-placement               dapr-system    True     Running  1
 0.11.2    1m    2020-10-18 20:49.40
```

```
   dapr-dashboard              dapr-system   True      Running  1
0.3.0     1m    2020-10-18 20:49.40
   dapr-operator               dapr-system   True      Running  1
0.11.2    1m    2020-10-18 20:49.40
   dapr-sidecar-injector  dapr-system   True      Running  1
0.11.2    1m    2020-10-18 20:49.40
   dapr-sentry                 dapr-system   True      Running  1
0.11.2    1m    2020-10-18 20:49.40
```

The dapr status -k command is equal to querying the currently running pods in the Kubernetes dapr-system **namespace** via the kubectl CLI:

```
PS C:\Repos\dapr-samples\chapter08> kubectl get pods -n dapr-
system -w
NAME                                              READY    STATUS
RESTARTS    AGE
dapr-dashboard-78557d579c-ngvqt                   1/1      Running   0
2m4s
dapr-operator-74cdb5fff9-7qt89                    1/1      Running   0
2m4s
dapr-placement-7b5bbdd95c-d6kmw                   1/1      Running   0
2m4s
dapr-sentry-65d64b7cd8-v7z9n                      1/1      Running   0
2m4s
dapr-sidecar-injector-7759b8b9c4-whvph            1/1      Running   0
2m4s
```

From the pods count in the preceding output, you will see that there is only one replica of each pod from the Dapr system services. However, this could change with the Highly Available deployment option of Dapr. For our development environment, it's OK to have just one replica since our cluster has a reduced number of nodes.

Alternatively, you can query the services by running in the dapr.system namespace:

```
PS C:\Repos\dapr-samples\chapter08> kubectl get services -n
dapr-system -w
NAME                     TYPE         CLUSTER-IP       EXTERNAL-IP
PORT(S)       AGE
dapr-api                 ClusterIP    10.0.110.101     <none>
80/TCP        5m8s
dapr-dashboard           ClusterIP    10.0.181.183     <none>
8080/TCP      5m8s
dapr-placement           ClusterIP    10.0.50.163      <none>
80/TCP        5m8s
dapr-sentry              ClusterIP    10.0.226.45      <none>
```

```
80/TCP        5m8s
dapr-sidecar-injector    ClusterIP    10.0.147.138    <none>
443/TCP       5m8s
```

You can also gather the same information from Azure portal, as shown in the following screenshot:

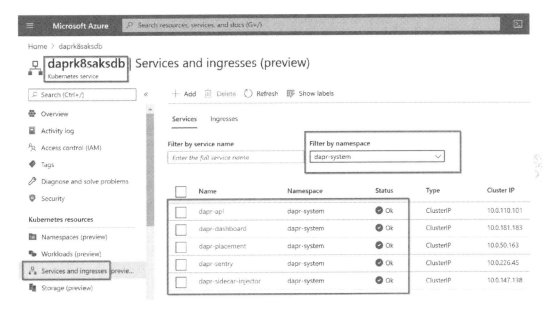

Figure 8.1 – Services by namespace in AKS

Here, you can see that **Services and ingresses** has been configured in AKS by status, filtered by namespace.

We can also leverage the Dapr dashboard here:

```
PS C:\Repos\dapr-samples\chapter08> dapr dashboard -k
Dapr dashboard found in namespace:    dapr-system
Dapr dashboard available at:    http://localhost:8080
```

With the `dapr dashboard -k` parameter, we can open the Dapr dashboard that's running in the Kubernetes environment. All of this is done inside the `dapr-system` namespace:

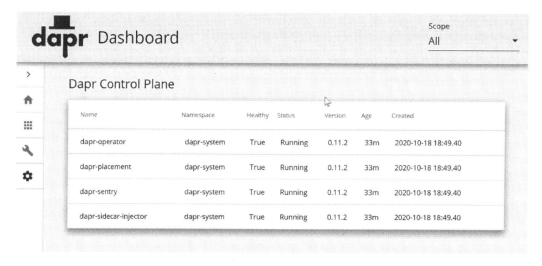

Figure 8.2 – Dapr dashboard in Kubernetes hosting mode

An overview of the various methods (kubectl, Azure portal, Dapr dashboard, and so on) we can use to gather feedback on the Dapr services running in Kubernetes is available here. The Kubernetes cluster is now ready to accept the deployment of a Dapr enabled application.

Deploying a Dapr application to Kubernetes

The service code for our Dapr application is now complete. However, we must package it so that it can be deployed to Kubernetes in a suitable manner. Our first objective is to publish these services as Docker containers.

The sample that's available for this chapter, `C:\Repos\dapr-samples\chapter08`, is aligned with the status we reached at the end of *Chapter 7, Using Actors*. To recap, the following are the Dapr applications that comprise our overall solution:

- `sample.microservice.order`
- `sample.microservice.reservation.service`
- `sample.microservice.reservationactor.service`
- `sample.microservice.customization`
- `sample.microservice.shipping`

There are other projects in this chapter's folder. However, the previous list only represents the Dapr applications that need to be built as docker images, which, for simplicity, are contained in separate folders with the same names and with matching `.proj` ASP.NET project files.

In the next section, we will start building the Docker images.

Building Docker images

As we intend to deploy our sample application to Kubernetes, the Docker container is the deployment format we must (and will) use.

> **Important note**
>
> For more information on how to publish ASP.NET Core with the Docker container format, I suggest that you read the documentation at `https://docs.microsoft.com/en-us/aspnet/core/host-and-deploy/docker/building-net-docker-images?view=aspnetcore-3.1`.

A Dockerfile is a text file that contains all the commands the Docker CLI needs to step through to build a Docker image. Let's start by examining the Dockerfile for the `sample.microservice.reservationactor.service` application:

```
FROM mcr.microsoft.com/dotnet/core/sdk:3.1 AS build
WORKDIR /src

COPY ["sample.microservice.reservationactor.interfaces/sample.
microservice.reservationactor.interfaces.csproj", "sample.
microservice.reservationactor.interfaces/"]
COPY ["sample.microservice.reservationactor.service/sample.
microservice.reservationactor.service.csproj", "sample.
microservice.reservationactor.service/"]
RUN dotnet restore "sample.microservice.reservationactor.
interfaces/sample.microservice.reservationactor.interfaces.
csproj"
RUN dotnet restore "sample.microservice.reservationactor.
service/sample.microservice.reservationactor.service.csproj"
COPY . .
WORKDIR "/src/sample.microservice.reservationactor.service"
RUN dotnet publish "sample.microservice.reservationactor.
service.csproj" -c Release -o /app/publish

FROM mcr.microsoft.com/dotnet/core/aspnet:3.1
```

```
WORKDIR /app
COPY --from=build /app/publish .
ENTRYPOINT ["dotnet", "sample.microservice.reservationactor.
service.dll"]
```

In the previous Dockerfile, there are several stages in the build process. Here, we can see that we are using two separate base images:

- `mcr.microsoft.com/dotnet/core/aspnet:3.1` is an image containing the ASP.NET Core and .NET Core runtimes and libraries. It is optimized for running ASP.NET Core in production.
- `mcr.microsoft.com/dotnet/core/sdk:3.1` contains the .NET Core CLI in addition to its runtime and is suitable for building ASP.NET Core projects.

First, a stage based on the `mcr.microsoft.com/dotnet/core/sdk:3.1` image is used as a destination for copying the involved projects, restoring the dependencies with `dotnet restore`, and then publishing them with `dotnet publish`.

In another, final, stage based on `mcr.microsoft.com/dotnet/core/aspnet:3.1`, the content of the `publish` output is copied into the root folder and `ENTRYPOINT` is declared to run the `dotnet` command on the project library once the container is started.

With the `docker build` command, you can execute all the steps in the dockerfile:

```
PS C:\Repos\dapr-samples\chapter08> docker build . -f .\sample.
microservice.reservationactor.service\Dockerfile -t sample.
microservice.reservationactor.service

Sending build context to Docker daemon  162.8kB
Step 1/13 : FROM mcr.microsoft.com/dotnet/core/sdk:3.1 AS build
 ---> 65279ad76723
Step 2/13 : WORKDIR /src
 ---> Using cache
 ---> a9f69c35a071

… omitted …
Step 9/13 : RUN dotnet publish "sample.microservice.
reservationactor.service.csproj" -c Release -o /app/publish
--no-restore
 ---> Using cache
 ---> ee9258e4f09c
Step 10/13 : FROM mcr.microsoft.com/dotnet/core/aspnet:3.1
 ---> e3559b2d50bb
Step 11/13 : WORKDIR /app
```

```
 ---> Using cache
 ---> 77e83b3972e8
Step 12/13 : COPY --from=build /app/publish .
 ---> Using cache
 ---> 225c199c1878
Step 13/13 : ENTRYPOINT ["dotnet", "sample.microservice.
reservationactor.service.dll"]
 ---> Using cache
 ---> d75448ddd469
Successfully built d75448ddd469
Successfully tagged sample.microservice.reservationactor.
service:latest
```

In the previous output, most of which has been omitted for brevity, it's worth noting that each of our Dockerfile instructions is evaluated as a numbered step: at the end, we have our ENTRYPOINT.

The build process with Docker must be performed for each of the Dapr applications we intend to deploy to Kubernetes.

We should now have our images built and available in our development machine. At this point, we need to publish them to a container image registry so that we can use them from our Kubernetes cluster.

Pushing Docker images

We are going to run our Dapr applications on the Kubernetes cluster. For this, we need to push the container images from our local environment to a location that is accessible by the Kubernetes cluster.

A Kubernetes cluster can retrieve the images from a **container registry**, which usually offers a private public and/or private container repository. A **container repository** is a collection of different versions of a container:

- DockerHub is a container registry for private or public repositories.
- Azure Container Registry is a private repository for containers running on Azure.
- Other container registry options can be available in private and public spaces.

I decided to use an Azure Container Registry because it fits well with the overall Azure-focused scenario. If you want, you can publish the sample containers to public or private repositories on DockerHub, or any other registry.

For a walkthrough on how to create an Azure Container Registry, please take a look at the documentation provided at `https://docs.microsoft.com/en-us/azure/container-registry/container-registry-get-started-portal`.

> **Important note**
>
> VS Code offers a rich developer experience when it comes to building Docker containers and pushing them to remote registries. Here, it makes sense to leverage these features while learning about something new, but it is highly recommended to integrate the container build's process into a CI/CD pipeline while leveraging GitHub, Azure DevOps, or any other platform suitable for the task.
>
> As a starting point, I suggest that you read this article by my colleague Jessica Tibaldi on a CI/CD approach to Dapr: `https://www.linkedin.com/pulse/s01e02-dapr-compass-how-we-organized-work-jessica-tibaldi/`.

If we examine our local environment, we should note that we have some new Docker container images. The following is a screenshot from VS Code:

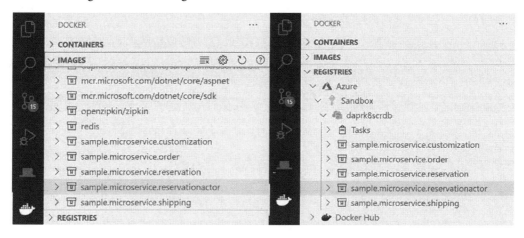

Figure 8.3 – Local images and Azure Container registry in VS Code

On the left-hand side of the preceding screenshot, we can see the images that are known by our Docker local environment. All of the container images we just built are present in this list, starting with the `sample.microservice.reservationactor.service` image that we analyzed in the previous section.

On the right-hand side of the preceding screenshot, we can see the destination of the container images: an Azure Container Registry.

The Azure extension in VS Code offers an integrated developer experience by easing authentication and access to our Azure resources: we can push the Docker images we just built to the Azure Container Registry with just a click. At `https://code.visualstudio.com/docs/containers/quickstart-container-registries`, you can find a step-by-step guide on how to complete it.

If we look at the integrated terminal windows in VS Code, we will see that the `docker push` command has been executed:

```
> Executing task: docker push daprk8scrdb.azurecr.io/sample.
microservice.reservationactor.service:latest <

The push refers to repository [daprk8scrdb.azurecr.io/sample.
microservice.reservationactor.service]
d513a9a5f622: Layer already exists
afc798cc7710: Layer already exists
049b0fdaa27c: Layer already exists
87e08e237115: Layer already exists
1915427dc1a4: Layer already exists
8a939c4fd477: Layer already exists
d0fe97fa8b8c: Layer already exists
latest: digest:
sha256:c6ff3b4058c98728318429ca49f0f8df0635f7efdfe3
4b6ccc7624fc3cea7d1e size: 1792
```

Some commands issued by the VS Code extension haven't been shown in the preceding output for brevity. With `docker tag`, an alias has been assigned that matches the Azure Container Registry address. So, here, our locally built `sample.microservice.reservationactor.service` can be referred to as a combination of `<ACR repository name>/<Docker image name>`

Each of the images we've built for the Dapr applications should now be pushed to the remote Azure Container Registry.

Once all the container images are available in the registry, we can proceed to deploying the Dapr applications to Kubernetes.

Managing secrets in Kubernetes

Secrets such as passwords, connection strings, and keys should always be kept separate from the rest of the code, as well as the configuration of a solution, since they could compromise its security if they're shared inappropriately.

Secret management is another building block of Dapr: integration is possible with many secret stores, such as Azure Key Vault, Hashicorp Vault, and Kubernetes itself. A full list is available at `https://docs.dapr.io/developing-applications/building-blocks/secrets/howto-secrets/`.

A Dapr application can retrieve secrets by invoking the Dapr API, which can be reached here:

```
GET http://localhost:<port>/v1.0/secrets/<vault>/<secret>
```

We can also use secrets to configure Dapr components, as documented in `https://docs.dapr.io/operations/components/component-secrets/`. In our sample solution, we are using an Azure Service Bus for the common pub/sub component and an Azure Cosmos DB for the state store of all the components. These rely on keys and connection strings we need to keep secure.

At this point, we need a secret store. Instead of creating another Azure resource, we can reach a compromise between complexity and another learning opportunity by adopting the Kubernetes built-in secret store, which is readily available via `kubectl`.

To create a secret via the kubectl CLI, we can use the `kubectl create secret` syntax, as described in the following code snippet:

```
kubectl create secret generic cosmosdb-secret --from-
literal=masterKey='#secret#' --from-literal=url='#secret#'

kubectl create secret generic servicebus-secret --from-literal=
connectionString='#secret#'
```

We can use the secrets from the Dapr component's `.yaml` files. For instance, the following is the actor state store component, which is mainly used by the `reservationactor-service` Dapr application:

```yaml
apiVersion: dapr.io/v1alpha1
kind: Component
metadata:
  name: reservationitemactorstore
  namespace: default
spec:
```

```yaml
type: state.azure.cosmosdb
metadata:
- name: url
  secretKeyRef:
    name: cosmosdb-secret
    key: url
- name: masterKey
  secretKeyRef:
    name: cosmosdb-secret
    key: masterKey
- name: database
  value: state
- name: collection
  value: reservationitemactorstate
- name: actorStateStore
  value: "true"
```

As you can see, instead of values being directly written in the `component-state-reservationitem.yaml` file for metadata, we reference the key's `url` and `masterKey` components from the secret; that is, `cosmosdb-secret`.

We must reference the secrets from all the Dapr component's configuration files. Once we've done that, we can start deploying our Dapr applications.

Deploying applications

So far, we have managed to push the Docker images for our Dapr applications to the Azure Container Registry. Before we can even attempt to deploy the applications, we need to connect them to the Azure Kubernetes Service.

From a Terminal window, we can launch the following command with the Azure CLI:

```
az aks update --name daprk8saksdb --resource-group daprk8srgdb
--attach-acr daprk8scrdb
```

Because we've launched the command in our Azure login context, it executes it. This means it has the correct access rights on both the AKS and the ACR.

As you may recall from the previous chapters, in Dapr's standalone hosting mode, we launched an application with the Dapr CLI, like this:

```
dapr run --app-id "reservationactor-service" --app-port "5004"
--dapr-grpc-port "50040" --dapr-http-port "5014" --components-
path components" -- dotnet run --project ./sample.microservice.
reservationactor.service/sample.microservice.reservationactor.
service.csproj --urls="http://+:5004"
```

In the Kubernetes hosting mode, we have to create a .yaml file configuration for the Dapr application and then apply it to Kubernetes.

The sample.microservice.reservationactor.yaml file that corresponds to the reservationactor-service Dapr application looks as follows:

```yaml
apiVersion: apps/v1
kind: Deployment
metadata:
  name: reservationactor-service
  namespace: default
  labels:
    app: reservationactor-service
spec:
  replicas: 1
  selector:
    matchLabels:
      app: reservationactor-service
  template:
    metadata:
      labels:
        app: reservationactor-service
      annotations:
        dapr.io/enabled: "true"
        dapr.io/id: "reservationactor-service"
        dapr.io/port: "80"
        dapr.io/config: "appconfig"
        dapr.io/log-level: "info"
    spec:
      containers:
      - name: reservationactor-service
        image: daprk8scrdb.azurecr.io/sample.microservice.
        reservationactor:latest
        ports:
        - containerPort: 80
        imagePullPolicy: Always
```

The previous snippet is a standard configuration file for a Kubernetes deployment. Note that the `daprk8scrdb.azurecr.io/sample.microservice. reservationactor` container image with the `latest` version is not specific to Dapr. The only portion that indicates the presence of Dapr is in the metadata annotations: `dapr.io/enabled: "true"` informs the Dapr services in Kubernetes that the Dapr sidecar container has been injected into this pod, granting it the ability to access the Dapr building blocks. The `dapr.io/id: "reservationactor-service"` annotation specifies the Dapr application's ID.

This is the overall, and minimal, impact Dapr has on an application deployed on Kubernetes. With `dapr dashboard -k`, we can see that all our Dapr applications have now been configured in Kubernetes.

Armed with the necessary components and applications files, we are now ready to deploy the solution to Kubernetes. The following are the commands we execute from the solution root folder, which in my case is `C:\Repos\dapr-samples\chapter08`:

```
kubectl apply -f .\Deploy\component-pubsub.yaml
kubectl apply -f .\Deploy\component-state-order.yaml
kubectl apply -f .\Deploy\component-state-reservation.yaml
kubectl apply -f .\Deploy\component-state-reservationitem.yaml
kubectl apply -f .\Deploy\component-state-shipping.yaml
kubectl apply -f .\Deploy\component-state-customization.yaml

kubectl apply -f .\Deploy\sample.microservice.order.yaml
kubectl apply -f .\Deploy\sample.microservice.reservation.yaml
kubectl apply -f .\Deploy\sample.microservice.reservationactor.
yaml
kubectl apply -f .\Deploy\sample.microservice.customization.
yaml
kubectl apply -f .\Deploy\sample.microservice.shipping.yaml
```

We can check the impact the new deployment has on Kubernetes from the Azure portal via kubectl or via the Dapr dashboard, as shown in the following screenshot:

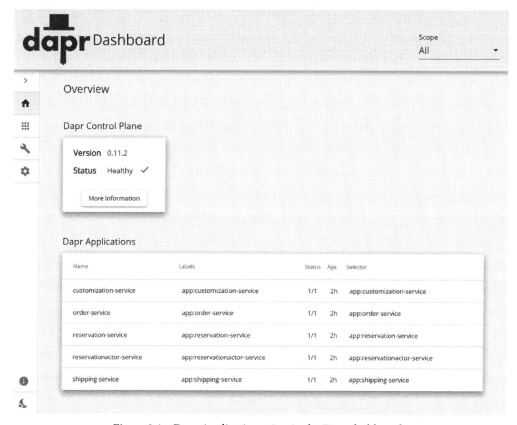

Figure 8.4 – Dapr Applications view in the Dapr dashboard

Here, we can see the list of Dapr applications that are available, shown by their Dapr application IDs. In the following screenshot, we can see the components from the Dapr dashboard:

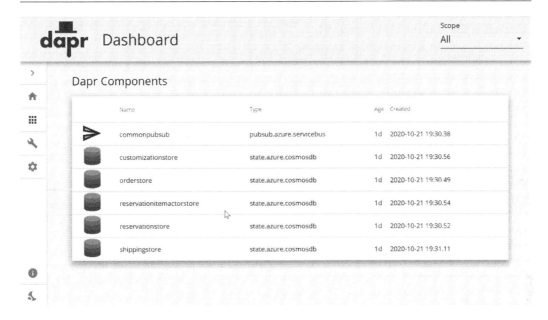

Figure 8.5 – Components view in the Dapr dashboard

Before we move on to the next section, let's verify the output of a Dapr application.
By using the `kubectl logs -f` command, we can follow the output log from any app
and container, in a similar fashion to what we did in the local development environment
via the Dapr CLI:

```
PS C:\Repos\dapr-samples\chapter08> kubectl logs -l
app=reservationactor-service -c reservationactor-service
--namespace default -f
Hosting environment: Production
Content root path: /app
Now listening on: http://[::]:80
Application started. Press Ctrl+C to shut down.
Activating actor id: rockiecookie
Actor: rockiecookie Activated
Balance of rockiecookie was 324, now 320
Activating actor id: bussola8
Actor: bussola8 Activated
Balance of bussola8 was 557, now 564
Activating actor id: bussola1
Actor: bussola1 Activated
Balance of bussola1 was 174, now 172
Activating actor id: crazycookie
Actor: crazycookie Activated
Balance of crazycookie was 32, now 30
```

The preceding output comes from the ASP.NET containers in the pods for the deployment corresponding to the `reservationactor-service` Dapr application. Here, we can see the Dapr Actors activating and the balance quantity being updated. This is the result of an order that was submitted to the `order-service` application, which activated the saga orchestration process we described in *Chapter 5, Publish and Subscribe*, helping it reach the `reservationactor-service` application.

You might be wondering, how could any test user reach the API exposed by `order-service`? No one can access it yet; I just wanted you to know how to read logs first. Before we move on, we need to learn how to expose our ASP.NET, Dapr-enabled application in Kubernetes. We'll do this in the next section.

Exposing Dapr applications to external clients

At this stage of deploying the *Biscotti Brutti Ma Buoni* backend solution to Kubernetes, we have all the Dapr components and applications properly configured. However, without the proper configurations, no external calls can reach any of our service APIs.

Our objective is to expose the ASP.NET endpoints of the Dapr applications, starting with `order-service`, so that we can invoke the `/order` API method from our development machine. The following diagram shows what we are trying to achieve:

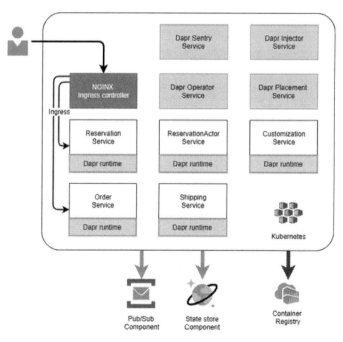

Figure 8.6 – The main components in a Kubernetes deployment

In the preceding diagram, the main Dapr services are depicted in Kubernetes alongside our Dapr applications. They are represented as pods containing the ASP.NET container, along with the service code and the Dapr sidecar.

We need to configure our Kubernetes cluster with an **ingress controller (IC)**. For this, we can use **NGINX**. A detailed step-by-step configuration is available in the Azure documentation at `https://docs.microsoft.com/en-us/azure/aks/ingress-basic`.

> **API management with Dapr**
>
> Dapr offers a powerful integration with **Azure API Management**. In this approach, instead of a generic ingress controller such as Nginx, the self-hosted gateway component of Azure API Management will run on pods in Kubernetes, directly integrated with Dapr, and managed via the API Management control plane.
>
> I suggest that you investigate this option for exposing APIs built with Dapr by reading the documentation at `https://docs.microsoft.com/en-us/azure/api-management/api-management-dapr-policies`.

For your convenience, the `Deploy\deploy-nginx.ps1` file contains all the steps, charted with **Helm**, for preparing the Nginx ingress controller and the ingresses according to our sample solution.

With the following command, we can verify that the ingress controller is ready and make note of its public IP (the `xy.zk.193.46` address you can see in the following code):

```
PS C:\Repos\dapr-samples\chapter08> kubectl --namespace
ingress-basic get services -o wide -w nginx-ingress-ingress-
ngin
x-controller
NAME                                          TYPE
CLUSTER-IP      EXTERNAL-IP      PORT(S)                       AGE
SELECTOR
nginx-ingress-ingress-nginx-controller    LoadBalancer
10.0.21.122    xy.zk.193.46    80:32732/TCP,443:30046/TCP    41h
app.kubernetes.io/component=controller,app.kubernetes.io/
instance=nginx-ingress,app.kubernetes.io/name=ingress-nginx
```

Once the ingress controller has been deployed, we have to configure an **ingress** to the **service**. By examining the `Deploy\sample.microservice.order.yaml` configuration file for `order-service`, which we have already applied to Kubernetes, we can observe the `Service` configuration:

```
...omitted...

---
apiVersion: v1
kind: Service
metadata:
  name: order-service
  namespace: default
spec:
  type: ClusterIP
  ports:
  - port: 80
  selector:
    app: order-service
```

The corresponding ingress for `order-service`, which is available in the `Deploy\ingress-order.yaml` file, is as follows:

```
apiVersion: networking.k8s.io/v1beta1
kind: Ingress
metadata:
  name: order-service-ingress
  namespace: default
  annotations:
    kubernetes.io/ingress.class: nginx
    nginx.ingress.kubernetes.io/ssl-redirect: "false"
    nginx.ingress.kubernetes.io/use-regex: "true"
    nginx.ingress.kubernetes.io/rewrite-target: /$1$2
spec:
  rules:
  - http:
      paths:
      - path: /bbmb/(order)+(.*)
        backend:
          serviceName: order-service
          servicePort: 80
```

From these two configurations, we can see that a resource of the `service` type for the `nginx` class, named `order-service`, has been used to configure the path in a resource of the `ingress` type.

What has been described so far for the Dapr application's `order-service` has to be applied to `reservation-service` too.

At this point, we should get an output that looks similar to the following:

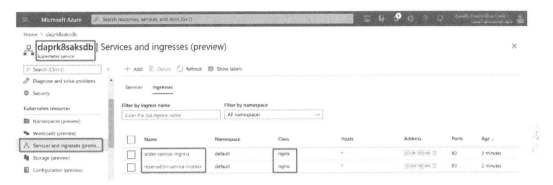

Figure 8.7 – AKS ingress resources view

Here, we can see the two `order-service-ingress` and `reservation-service-ingress` ingresses of the `nginx` class. While I obfuscated **Address** in my deployment, it is the same for the ingress controller, as expected.

We can run our manual test by invoking the HTTP endpoint via curl or the VS Code extension, as shown in the following code:

```
GET http://<omitted>.westeurope.cloudapp.azure.com/bbmb/
balance/crazycookie HTTP/1.1
###
POST http://<omitted>.westeurope.cloudapp.azure.com/bbmb/order
HTTP/1.1
... JSON payload ...
```

With our ingress controller, services, and ingress configured, we have gained access to the necessary ASP.NET endpoints from outside the AKS cluster.

Summary

This book has introduced you to the fictious eCommerce site *Biscotti Brutti Ma Buoni*, and over the course of the previous chapters, we have built prototypes for several microservices. Along the way, we've learned how the building blocks of Dapr enable any developer, using any language on any platform, to accelerate the development and deployment of a microservice architecture.

We have stayed focused on the building blocks of Dapr and how to combine them in an optimal way, always remaining in the context of the local development environment. We did this by relying on the Dapr standalone mode to test and debug our microservice code.

In this chapter, we finally shifted gear and moved toward a production-ready environment for our Dapr applications, such as a Kubernetes cluster. We learned how to configure Dapr on a Kubernetes cluster, as well as how to handle secrets, components, deploying applications, and ingress configuration.

Although we verified the proper configuration and operations we must perform on the Dapr application by following the logs from various services and pods, we did not approach the tracing capabilities of Dapr. As we prepare our solution so that it's production-ready, we need a well-organized and structured monitoring approach. This is what we are going to cover in the next chapter.

9
Tracing Dapr Applications

In this chapter, you will learn about the observability options in Dapr, by exploring how traces, logs, and metrics are emitted and can be collected in Dapr, using Zipkin, Prometheus, and Grafana. These are the main topics of the chapter:

- Observing applications in Dapr
- Tracing with Zipkin
- Analyzing metrics with Prometheus and Grafana

With Dapr in self-hosted mode, which we used during the development of our Dapr applications, we had the option to directly access the logs from the Dapr sidecar processes and applications as a console output, in addition to the ability to debug our service code with **Visual Studio Code (VS Code)**.

In the Kubernetes mode of Dapr, however, the approach is going to be different because of the complexity of a multi-node cluster and the constraints imposed on a production environment.

Technical requirements

The code for this sample can be found on GitHub at `https://github.com/PacktPublishing/Practical-Microservices-with-Dapr-and-.NET/tree/main/chapter09`.

In this chapter, the working area for scripts and code is expected to be found at `<repository path>\chapter09\`. In my local environment, it is to be found at `C:\Repos\dapr-samples\chapter09`.

Please refer to the *Setting up Dapr* section in *Chapter 1, Introducing Dapr* for a complete guide on the tools needed to develop with Dapr and work with the samples.

This chapter builds upon the Kubernetes cluster we set up and configured in *Chapter 8, Deploying to Kubernetes*: refer to that chapter to reach the same configuration.

Observing applications in Dapr

In a monolithic application made of few components running on a limited number of nodes, understanding how the application is behaving is a relatively simple task. In such a context, there is an expectation that by monitoring the activity of some processes, on one or maybe two nodes to get higher availability, and their usage of the node's CPU and memory over time, we can get a good perspective on the application's behavior. Log files would be available on the nodes, and the collection of those files could be arranged with any classic monitoring solution.

Once the number of working components increases dramatically, however, when we leverage the advantages coming from building microservices around business capabilities, the level of complexity grows along with it. We have more processes to monitor, and it is also likely that these are related to each other and might even have dependencies to external components: as we have learned throughout this book, microservices often collaborate together via a service-to-service invocation or publish/subscribe, and rely on state stores.

The complexity growth does not stop here: the life cycle of the microservices composing our solution is shorter; maybe we are able to scale out microservice instances by reacting to the current load. Our microservice solution will not necessarily need more nodes to run: being more expensive is not an objective! On the other hand, our solution might gain a significant benefit by operating on an infrastructure composed of many self-repairing nodes.

Moreover, the development and deployment practices we learned with Docker give us more flexibility but add an abstraction layer between the node and our code.
We will not understand much of our application's behavior by looking at metrics from any of the nodes.

From this increased (but, alas, necessary and welcome) complexity comes the need for observability of microservices: the ability to instrument new and existing applications to collect metrics, logs, and traces from a diverse set of processes, running on a variable number of hosts (nodes and containers), with the primary objective of correlating each signal with others, to offer a complete view of a client request or job.

Let's consider the following simplified representation of the saga pattern, introduced in *Chapter 5, Publish and Subscribe*:

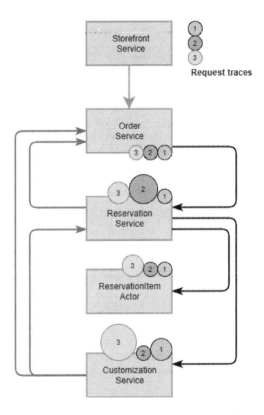

Figure 9.1 – Request traces in a microservice solution

As depicted in *Figure 9.1*, when our solution processes many requests by splitting the work among many microservices, how can we understand which requests are taking more time to execute? How do we account for the interaction between microservices and the state store? To simplify, the goal with observability is to gain a clear view on which request (out of **1**, **2**, or **3**) is consuming the most resources.

Dapr supports distributed tracing by automatically correlating traces of a request as it crosses boundaries between the Dapr runtime, our service code, and the Dapr services and components.

As Dapr is a runtime, you only need to configure tracing and where to export traces to, and you are done—no frameworks or packages to install and maintain.

Dapr also exposes metrics of the overall Dapr infrastructure, from runtime in sidecar containers to system services, offering full visibility of how Dapr operates on the Kubernetes (or self-hosted) environment.

> **Important note: OpenTelemetry**
>
> Dapr adopts **OpenTelemetry** (see `https://opentelemetry.io/` to learn more), a **Cloud Native Computing Foundation** (**CNCF**) project with the goal to facilitate integration with frameworks and tools for tracing, metrics, and logs. With the **Tracing Exporters** components, Dapr is able to export traces with OpenTelemetry-integrated tools and platforms.

In the next section, we will set up Zipkin to see how distributed tracing can help us understand how our Dapr applications are performing.

Tracing with Zipkin

Zipkin is an open source distributed tracing system. It offers the ability to search for traces by ID, service, operation, or tags, and shows the dependencies between services. You can learn more at `https://zipkin.io/`.

These are the steps we will follow to set up Zipkin in Dapr on Kubernetes:

1. Setting up Zipkin
2. Configuring the Dapr exporter
3. Enabling tracing in Dapr
4. Investigating with Zipkin

Let's start by installing Zipkin in the cluster we prepared in *Chapter 8*, *Deploying to Kubernetes*.

Setting up Zipkin

Zipkin is distributed as a Docker container. You probably already have it on your local development environment, as it has been installed by default with Dapr.

We can deploy it to Kubernetes with the following `C:\Repos\dapr-samples\chapter09\Deploy\zipkin.yaml` file which has the following code:

```yaml
apiVersion: apps/v1
kind: Deployment
metadata:
    name: zipkin
    labels:
        app: zipkin
spec:
    replicas: 1
    selector:
        matchLabels:
            app: zipkin
    template:
        metadata:
            labels:
                app: zipkin
        spec:
            containers:
            - name: zipkin
              image: openzipkin/zipkin
              ports:
              - containerPort: 9411
---
apiVersion: v1
kind: Service
metadata:
    name: zipkin
    namespace: default
    labels:
        app: zipkin
spec:
    type: ClusterIP
    ports:
    - protocol: TCP
      port: 9411
      targetPort: 9411
    selector:
        app: zipkin
```

In the previous code snippet, Zipkin is deployed with the `openzipkin/zipkin` container exposed at port `9411` and a service endpoint is created, with the same port. This is necessary to make it reachable by service name from other pods.

We can apply the configuration to Kubernetes with the following command:

```
kubectl apply -f .\Deploy\zipkin.yaml
```

To access Zipkin on Kubernetes we have two options: as we have a NGINX ingress controller already configured in our cluster, we could create an ingress to the Zipkin service and restrict access to the path from our client IP address; alternatively, we could use the port-forwarding command of kubectl, as in the following command:

```
kubectl port-forward svc/zipkin 9412:9411
```

With the kubectl port-forward command, a local port on our development environment is mapped to a service (this could also be a pod) on Kubernetes. As I already have Zipkin locally, I mapped the local port 9412 to port 9411 on the service named zipkin in Kubernetes.

If we access the Zipkin portal at http://localhost:9412/ there should be no data, as we still need to configure Dapr to export data to Zipkin: we'll do this in the next step.

Configuring the Dapr exporter

As we installed Zipkin, we must now configure Dapr to send all distributed traces to it.

We have to create a Dapr component, similarly to what we did with the publish/subscribe and state stores. The C:\Repos\dapr-samples\chapter09\Deploy\component-zipkin.yaml content is the following:

```
apiVersion: dapr.io/v1alpha1
kind: Component
metadata:
   name: zipkin
   namespace: default
spec:
   type: exporters.zipkin
   metadata:
   - name: enabled
     value: "true"
   - name: exporterAddress
     value: "http://zipkin.default.svc.cluster.local:9411/
     api/v2/spans"
```

The component of type exporters.zipkin exports data to the Kubernetes service named zipkin in the default namespace.

Let's apply it with the following command:

```
kubectl apply -f .\Deploy\component-zipkin.yaml
```

We can check that the component has been configured from the Dapr dashboard, as illustrated in the following screenshot:

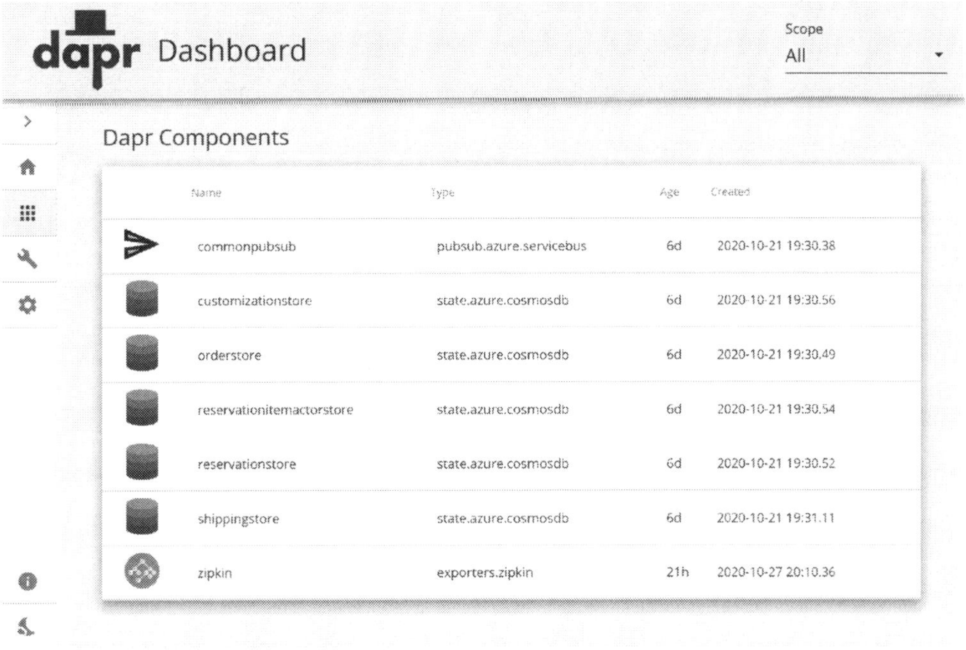

Figure 9.2 – Zipkin in Dapr components

In *Figure 9.2*, we can verify that the component for Zipkin is recognized by Dapr; next, we will enable tracing in our Dapr applications.

Enabling tracing in Dapr

At this stage, Zipkin is working in Kubernetes, and Dapr is configured to export distributed traces to it. As a last step, we need to start the flow of traces from the Dapr applications.

The `\Deploy\configuration-zipkin.yaml` file has a Dapr configuration suitable for our need, as illustrated in the following code snippet:

```
apiVersion: dapr.io/v1alpha1
kind: Configuration
metadata:
```

```
    name:  tracing
    namespace:  default
spec:
    tracing:
        samplingRate:  "1"
    mtls:
        enabled:  true
        workloadCertTTL:  24h
        allowedClockSkew:  15m
```

In the previous snippet, samplingRate is configured: as the value is > 0, tracing is enabled; and with value = 1, all traces get sampled. You can check the Dapr documentation at https://docs.dapr.io/operations/configuration/ configuration-overview/#tracing to learn more.

We apply the configuration with the following command:

```
kubectl  apply  -f  .\Deploy\configuration-zipkin.yaml
```

We now need to update our Dapr applications with the new configuration, as we do in the following example:

```
apiVersion:  apps/v1
kind: Deployment
metadata:
    name:  reservation-service
    namespace:  default
    labels:
        app:  reservation-service
spec:
    ... omitted ...
    template:
        metadata:
            labels:
                app:  reservation-service
            annotations:
                dapr.io/enabled:  "true"
                dapr.io/id:  "reservation-service"
                dapr.io/port:  "80"
                dapr.io/config:  "tracing"
... omitted ...
```

The change to dapr.io/config annotation must be replicated on each of our Dapr applications' .yaml files, as follows:

```
kubectl   apply   -f   .\Deploy\sample.microservice.order.yaml
kubectl   apply   -f   .\Deploy\sample.microservice.reservation.
yaml
kubectl   apply   -f   .\Deploy\sample.microservice.
reservationactor.yaml
kubectl   apply   -f   .\Deploy\sample.microservice.customization.
yaml
kubectl   apply   -f   .\Deploy\sample.microservice.shipping.yaml
```

With the previous kubectl commands, we re-apply the deployments of our Dapr applications in Kubernetes, updated to the new Dapr configuration.

The Dapr dashboard offers a nice view of the configuration, as shown in the following screenshot:

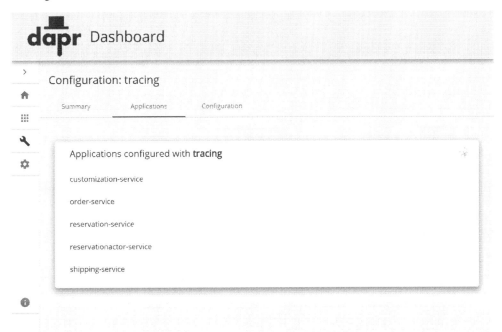

Figure 9.3 – Dapr application adopting tracing

In *Figure 9.3*, we see the **Configuration** named **tracing** and the applications configured with it: each of the Dapr applications in the scope of our solution has tracing enabled.

It is time we learn how Zipkin can help us in understanding our applications' behavior.

Investigating with Zipkin

We need some data to visualize in Zipkin: the `order.test.http` file you can use in VS Code with the `RestClient` extension is a simple approach to perform sample `http` requests.

By requesting GET `http://<your AKS cluster>/bbmb/balance/` and POST `http://<your AKS cluster>/bbmb/order/` a few times, we should generate enough traces to examine in Zipkin.

Let's open the Zipkin portal at `http://localhost:9412/` or whichever local port we are using with port forwarding. Take a look at the following screenshot:

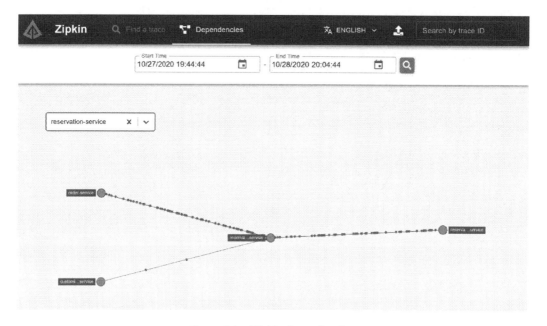

Figure 9.4 – Zipkin dependencies

In *Figure 9.4*, let's examine the **Dependencies** first, and let's select the service named `reservation-service`, which takes a central position in the flow of interactions in our solution: we should have a similar view with many points (each symbolizing an interaction) from `order-service` to `reservation-service`, many more from here to `reservationactor-service`, and fewer to `customization-service`. Many of the interactions between `reservationactor-service` to `customization-service` are represented with a red color, so it is reasonable to ask: what is going on?

If we used the `order.test.http` file to simulate requests to our Dapr solution, we would have been ordering and requesting the customization of the infamous cookie with **stock-keeping unit (SKU) crazycookie**: we introduced in *Chapter 5, Publish and Subscribe*, this fixed rule to simulate an unrecoverable error during the customization phase of the **saga pattern** we implemented.

Before we switch to the trace analysis in Zipkin, let's clarify two concepts: a **span** is the unit of work executed in a component or service, while a **trace** is a collection of spans. Take a look at the following screenshot:

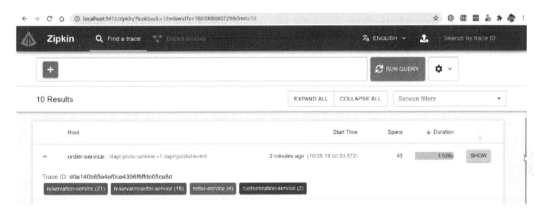

Figure 9.5 – Zipkin traces

In *Figure 9.5*, I managed to find a trace, originating from `order-service`. If I expand it, I see it includes interactions with all the other Dapr applications: it seems a good candidate for further investigation. By clicking **SHOW**, the Zipkin portal switches to a detailed view of all the spans in the trace.

We should get a view like the one in the following screenshot:

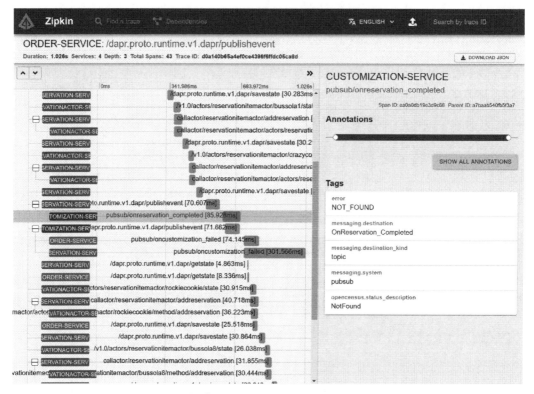

Figure 9.6 – Zipkin trace: NOT_FOUND error in a span

In *Figure 9.6*, we see the spans displayed in order, showing the service originating the span, the operation, and its execution time.

Let's focus on a span from customization-service, which is represented with the color red to evidence a failure.

In this span, Dapr reports that an error of type NOT_FOUND has been received while processing a call to pubsub/OnReservation_Completed.

To understand the interaction between Dapr and our code, we need to look at the ASP. NET controller in the project for the customization-service Dapr application, specifically the \sample.microservice.customization\Controllers\ CustomizationController.cs file, which you will find in the chapter09 folder.

Examining the code, we should find the portion in which customization-service simulates an error, once a cookie with the SKU **crazycookie** is requested by a customer. If the customization fails, our code does the following:

```
if  (!customizedItem.Succeeded)
{
        await  daprClient.
        PublishEventAsync<OrderCustomization>(PubSub,
        common.Topics.CustomizationFailedTopicName,result);

        Console.WriteLine($"Customization  in  {order.Id}
        of  {SKU}  for  {quantity}  failed");
        return  this.NotFound();
}
```

In the previous code snippet, the ASP.NET controller code is returning a NotFound result to the caller, just after it publishes a message to the OnCustomization_Failed topic via the configured Dapr publish/subscribe component—in our case, it is the **Azure Service Bus**.

Our choice in handling the irreversible error that customer-service encountered (or simulated) explains the NotFound error in the span we see in Zipkin. It also explains the next span we see in order, which is the notification of a failure to the next stages of the saga. Take a look at the following screenshot:

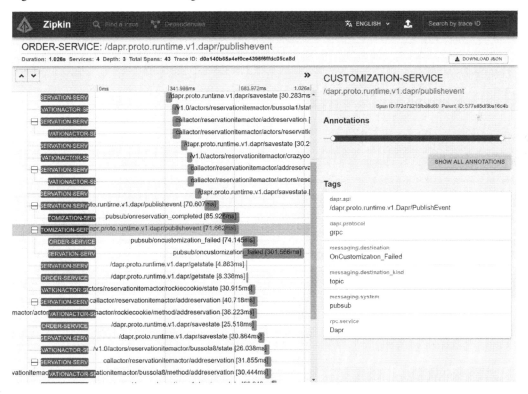

Figure 9.7 – Zipkin trace: span showing a publishevent action

Just to refresh on some of the concepts we learned so far, from *Figure 9.7* we see a span with a call to the Dapr **application programming interface (API)**, using the gRPC protocol: it is the Dapr **software development kit (SDK)** for ASP.NET, which relies on gRPC to interact with the Dapr sidecar container.

We've learned how to enable distributed tracing in our Dapr applications, and how to configure Zipkin to help us understand how our application is handling requests and events in complex interactions, as we saw with the saga example.

In the next part of the chapter, we will learn to monitor all the elements of Dapr, and about how they consume resources in a Kubernetes cluster, with Prometheus and Grafana.

Analyzing metrics with Prometheus and Grafana

Prometheus is an open source system and monitoring toolkit, a project with a long history that started in 2012 and is now part of the CNCF.

In our scenario here, we will use Prometheus to scrape the metrics exposed by all Dapr pods, and store them as time-series. It will act as the data source for the Grafana dashboards.

Grafana is an open source visualization and analytics tool. We will use it to examine the Dapr metrics by importing the dashboard templates released by the Dapr project as assets from `https://github.com/dapr/dapr/releases/`.

These are the steps we will follow:

1. Installing Prometheus
2. Installing Grafana
3. Importing dashboards

Let's start by installing the Prometheus service components.

Installing Prometheus

As described in the Dapr documentation, available at `https://docs.dapr.io/operations/monitoring/prometheus/`, we should first create a namespace to be used by Prometheus and Grafana, as follows:

```
kubectl create namespace dapr-monitoring
```

We are going to use Helm to install the charts for Prometheus and Grafana in the dapr-monitoring namespace, as illustrated in the following code snippet:

```
helm repo add prometheus-community https://prometheus-
community.github.io/helm-charts
helm  repo  update
helm install dapr-prom prometheus-community/prometheus -n dapr-
monitoring
```

The deployment could take some time, so let's proceed to the next command after all the pods are ready, as follows:

```
kubectl  get  pods  -n  dapr-monitoring -w
NAME                                                      READY
STATUS
dapr-prom-kube-state-metrics-7b5b859f9b-sjn5x             1/1
Running
dapr-prom-prometheus-alertmanager-676c85b59-58n77         2/2
Running
dapr-prom-prometheus-node-exporter-6tt72                  1/1
Running
dapr-prom-prometheus-node-exporter-9n8xf                  1/1
Running
dapr-prom-prometheus-node-exporter-k6bpm                  1/1
Running
dapr-prom-prometheus-pushgateway-d5d9dbbfc-7cpj6          1/1
Running
dapr-prom-prometheus-server-57fbcb9446-8r6rv              2/2
Running
```

The Prometheus pods are now running; before we move on to Grafana, let's collect the information of the Prometheus service address, as indicated by running the following command:

```
kubectl get svc -n dapr-monitoring
NAME                                  TYPE        CLUSTER-IP
dapr-prom-kube-state-metrics          ClusterIP   10.0.176.113
dapr-prom-prometheus-alertmanager     ClusterIP   10.0.122.126
dapr-prom-prometheus-node-exporter    ClusterIP   None
dapr-prom-prometheus-pushgateway      ClusterIP   10.0.219.150
dapr-prom-prometheus-server           ClusterIP   10.0.222.218
```

The service is named dapr-prom-prometheus-server: we will use this information to configure the Grafana data source in the following section.

Installing Grafana

Following the Dapr documentation at `https://docs.dapr.io/operations/monitoring/grafana/`, the command to install it is the following:

```
helm repo add grafana https://grafana.github.io/helm-chartshelm
repo update helm
```
```
install grafana grafana/grafana -n dapr-monitoring
```

As we are using PowerShell, we can obtain the password, autogenerated for us by Grafana, with the following command:

```
$base64secret = kubectl get secret --namespace dapr-
monitoring grafana -o jsonpath="{.data.admin-password}"
$password = [System.Text.Encoding]::UTF8.GetString([System.
Convert]::FromBase64String($base64secret))
$password

MIDoEFh8YtnfQLByAvG4vB1N4AVqk8I60v6jmogx
```

The last value from the previous output is the password—in my case, to access the Grafana dashboard.

We can now access the Grafana dashboard by port forwarding to the corresponding Kubernetes service.

Importing dashboards

We can access Grafana from our local development environment with the following command, mapping local port `8090` (as port `8080` is used by the Dapr dashboard by default), to the remote port `80`, like this:

```
kubectl port-forward svc/grafana 8090:80 -n dapr-
monitoring
```

By accessing `http://localhost:8090/` and submitting the credentials (the password from the previous section and the default username `admin`), we can log in to Grafana.

Once we access the Grafana portal **user interface** (**UI**), we need to add the Prometheus data source first, selecting the **Configuration** dial from the sidebar and then **Data Sources**, as illustrated in the following screenshot:

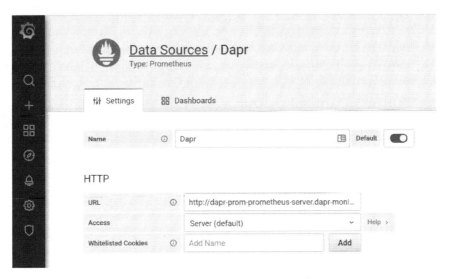

Figure 9.8 – Dapr data source in Grafana

As in *Figure 9.8*, we added the `http://dapr-prom-prometheus-server.dapr-monitoring` Prometheus service as a data source in Grafana, making it the default one.

We can import the following three ready-to-use dashboards provided by Dapr:

- `grafana-system-services-dashboard.json`
- `grafana-sidecar-dashboard.json`
- `grafana-actor-dashboard.json`

Each Dapr release has these dashboards as assets: for version 0.11.3, we can find the dashboards at `https://github.com/dapr/dapr/releases/tag/v0.11.3`.

We can import each one by adding it from the **Create** dial from the sidebar, selecting **Import**, and using the **URL** for the dashboard as the source.

The following screenshot shows the **Dapr System Services Dashboard** in Grafana:

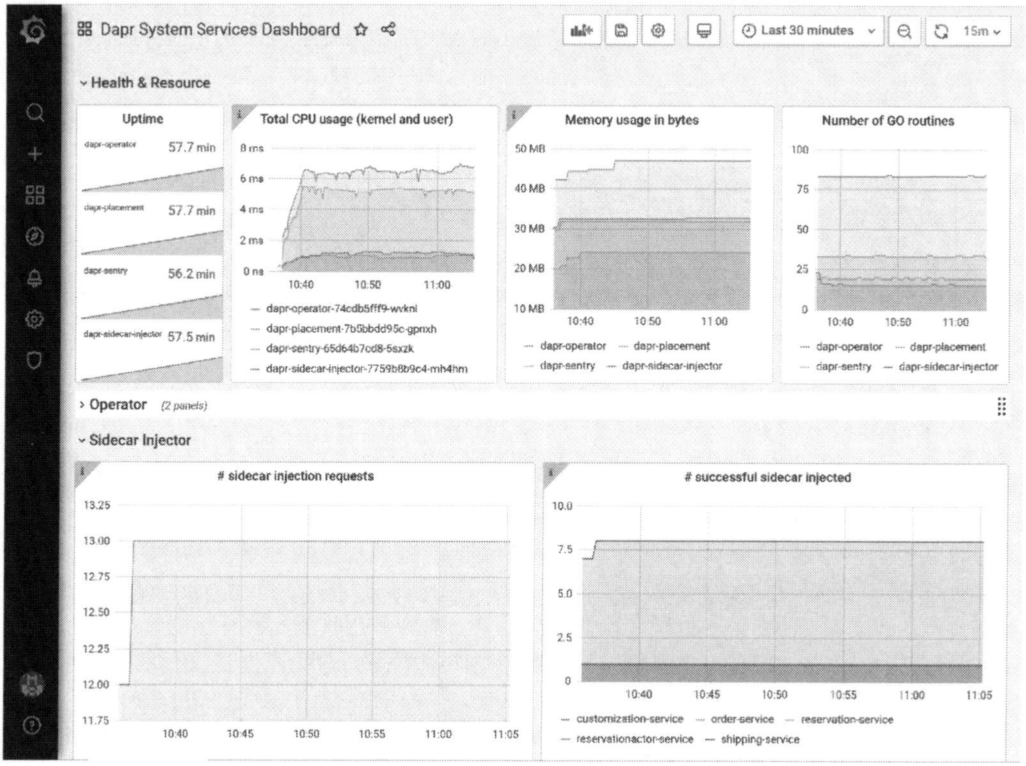

Figure 9.9 – Dapr System Services Dashboard in Grafana

At this stage, with Prometheus and Grafana running, we can start exploring the metrics exposed by Dapr. In *Figure 9.9*, we see the system services, with the total CPU and memory used by all Dapr services spread over the various nodes. Similar views are offered for actors and sidecars.

As our solution is not used by external users yet there is not much activity, other than the one we can simulate by ourselves sending a few requests to the API: in the next chapter, *Chapter 10, Load Testing and Scaling Dapr*, we will simulate more activity with load testing tools.

With Prometheus and Grafana we gained full visibility on how Dapr, from the runtime running in the sidecar of our applications' pods to the system services, behaves on Kubernetes.

Summary

In this chapter, we learned how observability, as provided by Dapr, brings order to the chaotic way a modern cloud native application could look, if approached with classic tools.

By understanding how Zipkin can help us analyze how our Dapr applications behave in a complex environment, such as Kubernetes. We now have the confidence we need to face the brave new world of cloud native applications.

With Prometheus and Grafana, we learned how Dapr informs developers and operators how the application is performing on Kubernetes, whether this is a cloud implementation, on-premises, or on the edge.

In the next chapter, we will leverage these abilities to observe how Dapr and our applications react to a heavy user load.

10
Load Testing and Scaling Dapr

In this chapter, we will learn how to scale Dapr applications in a Kubernetes environment and how to load test a Dapr solution by simulating user behaviors with the Locust testing tool.

In this chapter, we will cover the following topics:

- Scaling Dapr in Kubernetes
- Load testing with Locust
- Load testing Dapr
- Autoscaling with KEDA

Load testing is an important practice in software development. It offers developers and operators a scientific approach, guided by practices and tools, to finding the best possible answer to various questions, such as how will this application react to an increase of requests? At which point will the application's response start degrading in terms of success rate and response time? Will the infrastructure be able to sustain a specific rate of requests with certain performances with the allocated resources?

These questions explore both the technical and economic side of our architecture: in a cloud-native architecture, the operational cost is a factor that can and should influence the design. The knowledge you will gain in this chapter will enable you to perform load testing on your Dapr application and to adjust the infrastructure to your business needs.

Technical requirements

The code for this chapter's examples can be found in this book's GitHub repository at `https://github.com/PacktPublishing/Practical-Microservices-with-Dapr-and-.NET/tree/main/chapter10`.

In this chapter, the working area for scripts and code is `<repository path>\chapter10\`. In my local environment, it is `C:\Repos\dapr-samples\chapter10`.

Please refer to the *Setting up Dapr* section of *Chapter 1, Introducing Dapr,* for a complete guide on the tools you will need to develop with Dapr and work with the examples in this chapter.

There are some additional requirements you will need to accomplish the goals of this chapter. Let's take a look.

Bash

In this chapter, we are going to deploy Azure resources using a shell script.

One option is to install and use the **Windows Subsystem for Linux** (**WSL2**) on Windows 10, by following the instructions at `https://docs.microsoft.com/en-us/windows/wsl/install-win10`.

An alternative to installing WSL2 locally is to rely on Azure Cloud Shell, as described in `https://docs.microsoft.com/en-us/azure/cloud-shell/quickstart`, and launch the deployment from the context of Azure Cloud Shell.

Python

Python version 3.6 or later is required if you intend to install and try Locust on your local development machine.

If this version is not already installed on your environment, you can follow the instructions for Python 3 on Windows at `https://docs.python-guide.org/starting/installation/`.

A quick way to verify whether you have Python 3 installed is to input the following in a Windows terminal:

```
PS C:\Repos\dapr-samples\chapter10> python --version
Python 3.8.6
```

If you decide to use Python from the **WSL2**, you should follow the instructions for Python 3 on Linux at https://docs.python-guide.org/starting/installation/. A quick way to verify whether you have Python 3 installed is to input the following in a Windows terminal:

```
master@DB-SURFACEBOOK2:/c/Repos/dapr-samples/chapter10$ python3
--version
Python 3.6.9
```

As shown in the preceding output, the version of Python 3 that's installed on your version of Windows could be different than the one that's available in WSL2.

Locust

I suggest that you install Locust on your local development machine to verify the tests before publishing them to a Locust swarm.

The installation guide for Locust is available at https://docs.locust.io/en/stable/installation.html.

If you decided to use Python from Windows, use the following command to install Locust from a Windows terminal:

```
PS C:\Repos\dapr-samples\chapter10> pip3 install locust
```

To verify the installation and version of Locust, you can use the following command:

```
PS C:\Repos\dapr-samples\chapter10> locust -V
locust 1.3.1
```

If you decide to use Python from the WSL2, the same context applies to the installation of Locust:

```
master@DB-SURFACEBOOK2:/c/Repos/dapr-samples/chapter10$ pip3
install locust
```

Locust should be installed in the same environment. This is how you verify the Locust version in WSL2:

```
master@DB-SURFACEBOOK2:/c/Repos/dapr-samples/chapter10$ locust
-V
locust 1.3.1
```

Next, let us have a look at the Kuberneted configuration.

Kubernetes configuration

This chapter builds upon the Kubernetes cluster we set up and configured in *Chapter 8, Deploying to Kubernetes*. Please refer to this chapter to ensure you have the same configuration.

The monitoring configuration we prepared with **Zipkin**, **Prometheus**, and **Grafana** in *Chapter 9, Tracing Dapr Applications*, is also useful, even if it's not necessary to follow the instructions. Please refer to this chapter if you want to benefit from the same configuration.

Scaling Dapr on Kubernetes

In the world of monolithic architectures, the compute and memory resources available to an application are constrained by the hosts that it operates on; that is, VMs or physical nodes. For such applications, it becomes an extraordinary challenge to distribute requests and jobs evenly between multiple hosts. They often resort to an active/passive mode in which only a portion of the allocated resources benefit the application, while the rest are passively sitting idle, waiting for a failure of the active environment so that they can switch from their passive role to an active one.

The following diagram depicts the challenges of scaling monolithic applications:

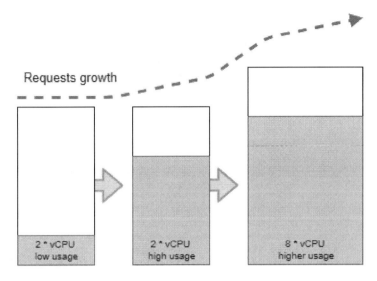

Figure 10.1 – Scaling monolithic applications

Given these factors, in order to respond to an increase of client requests, which translates to a demand for more computing resources, the response is often to scale up the resources. This can be done by substituting the hosts with more powerful ones, as shown in the preceding diagram. This approach is deemed to inefficiently support workloads with an elastic demand for resources over time.

In the context of microservice architectures, the application is designed with many more components that can be independently deployed and scaled. At any time, there could be multiple instances of a microservice running on different hosts.

For an application based on microservices, **scaling** means reacting to an increase or decrease in resource demand by adding or removing instances of the involved microservices. There is an expectation that the underlying hosting platform offers an elastic pool of resources, as depicted in the following diagram:

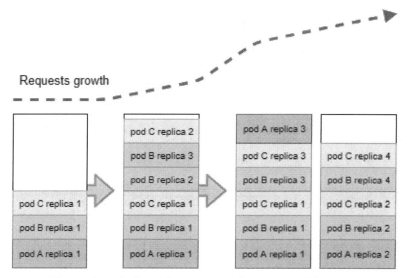

Figure 10.2 – Scaling microservice applications on Kubernetes

As we can see, our Dapr applications are executed as **pods**, the smallest deployable unit of computing in Kubernetes. We will rely on the features of this powerful orchestrator to scale our microservices.

Moving forward, the following are the concepts we can use to control scaling in Kubernetes:

- Replicas
- Autoscale
- Resource requests and limits

Let's start by exploring the concept of replicas in Kubernetes.

Replicas

In the context of Kubernetes, scaling translates to increasing the number of pod instances. Each Dapr application (or any application meant to be deployed on Kubernetes) is configured as a **deployment** with a number of **replicas**: this influences the number of **pods** that get created, each with an instance of a **container** of the application and, in terms of Dapr, a **sidecar**.

One of the benefits of Kubernetes is that you can quickly recover in case of application errors or availability issues with the hosts. We would want to keep our application responsive, even while its components are being recovered. So, in a production-ready environment, we will have more than one replica of each of our microservices: if one fails, the other replica will continue to respond to requests.

The deployments we've used so far have a replica value of 1: only one pod per Dapr application has been created. This simplifies the initial setup and configuration of any application on Kubernetes, but it is unlikely to stay at 1 once the solution is ready to enter production.

The following is an extract from the `\Deploy\sample.microservice.order.yaml` development file for the `order-service` application:

```
apiVersion: apps/v1
kind: Deployment
metadata:
  name: order-service
  namespace: default
  labels:
    app: order-service
spec:
  replicas: 1
...omitted...
```

Notice that the `replicas` value is 1. This might seem contradictory, but let's leave this value as we found it: we will affect it by enabling the autoscale mechanisms offered by Kubernetes.

Autoscale

In Kubernetes, we can manually change the replicas of a deployment by updating its configuration or by changing the number of nodes that support the cluster.

Kubernetes has the ability to automatically scale up and down the number of replicas of a deployment, based on the resource usage metrics of its pods, with the **Horizontal Pod Autoscaler** (**HPA**).

Kubernetes can also add or remove cluster nodes, depending on the overall resource's capacity and demand. If there are more pods to spin up than the available CPUs, the **Cluster Autoscaler** (**CA**) can sense it and accommodate the request by adding a new node.

The two Kubernetes autoscalers often operate in tandem: the first by requesting more replicas for a deployment under increasing load, the second by adapting the cluster size to the overall resource demands by pods.

You can find more information about these Kubernetes features at `https://kubernetes.io/docs/tasks/run-application/horizontal-pod-autoscale/` and from an Azure Kubernetes Service perspective at `https://docs.microsoft.com/en-us/azure/aks/concepts-scale`.

To avoid introducing too much complexity all at once, we will focus on the Horizontal Pod Autoscaler. There is a valid walkthrough available at `https://docs.microsoft.com/en-us/azure/aks/tutorial-kubernetes-scale#autoscale-pods`.

The following are the changes we intend to apply to each of our Dapr application deployments, starting with `\Deploy\sample.microservice.order.yaml` for `order-service`:

```
… omitted …
---
apiVersion: autoscaling/v1
kind: HorizontalPodAutoscaler
metadata:
  name: order-service-hpa
  namespace: default
spec:
  maxReplicas: 4
  minReplicas: 1
  scaleTargetRef:
    apiVersion: apps/v1
    kind: Deployment
    name: order-service
  targetCPUUtilizationPercentage: 50
```

In the previous configuration snippet, we configured a `HorizontalPodAutoscaler` resource so that it scales the replica of `Deployment`, named `order-service`, from a `minReplicas` value of 1 to a `maxReplicas` of 4, one replica at a time, if the deployment's resource usage exceeds the `targetCPUUtilizationPercentage` metric of 50%.

However, we are missing an important configuration element of our Dapr application's deployment: we must specify the resource requests and limits of our pods because otherwise, nobody will be able to understand it.

Resource requests and limits

Specifying requests and limits to CPU and memory usage is a good practice to allow for proper resource planning in Kubernetes. This prevents your pods from consuming all the resources available on the nodes, which subsequently impacts other pods in your solution or other systems running in the same cluster. However, this results in instability issues being created for your available nodes and workloads.

By setting resource requests and limits, we inform the Kubernetes cluster of how to properly handle our workload and the basis on which to scale it.

The pods of our Dapr application have two containers: the Dapr sidecar and our service code, based on the ASP.NET Core container image.

For the CPU and memory requests and limits of our ASP.NET service code, we need to make some initial assumptions that are suitable for a sample we have to assess. The Dapr documentation at `https://docs.dapr.io/operations/hosting/kubernetes/kubernetes-production/#sidecar-resource-requirements` suggests having a configuration that's suitable for the Dapr sidecar container in a production environment.

These settings can be applied to a Dapr application deployment as annotations. The following `\Deploy\sample.microservice.order.yaml` file for `order-service` shows the intended changes:

```
apiVersion: apps/v1
kind: Deployment
metadata:
  name: order-service
  namespace: default
  labels:
    app: order-service
spec:
  replicas: 1
  selector:
    matchLabels:
      app: order-service
  template:
    metadata:
      labels:
        app: order-service
      annotations:
        dapr.io/enabled: "true"
        dapr.io/id: "order-service"
        dapr.io/port: "80"
```

```
            dapr.io/config: "tracing"
            dapr.io/log-level: "info"
            dapr.io/sidecar-memory-request: "250Mi"
            dapr.io/sidecar-cpu-request: "100m"
            dapr.io/sidecar-memory-limit: "4000Mi"
            dapr.io/sidecar-cpu-limit: "1"
            dapr.io/sidecar-liveness-probe-period-seconds: "20"
            dapr.io/sidecar-readiness-probe-period-seconds: "20"
    spec:
      containers:
      - name: order-service
        image: daprk8scrdb.azurecr.io/sample.microservice.
        order:latest
        ports:
        - containerPort: 80
        imagePullPolicy: Always
        resources:
          limits:
            memory: "800Mi"
            cpu: "400m"
          requests:
            memory: "200Mi"
            cpu: "100m"
```
… omitted …

With dapr.io/sidecar-memory-request and dapr.io/sidecar-cpu-request, we specify that the Dapr sidecar in a pod for order-service should start by requesting 250 MiB of memory and 100 m of CPU (0.1 vCPU).

The container that contains our service code, which is using the daprk8scrdb.azurecr.io/sample.microservice.order:latest image, is requesting 100 MiB of memory and 100 m of CPU.

The Dapr sidecar has much higher resource limits than our service code since it's going to handle most of the I/O for our application.

Note

See https://kubernetes.io/docs/concepts/configuration/manage-resources-containers/#resource-units-in-kubernetes for more information on the units of measure used in Kubernetes.

Once we are done, we can apply the configuration:

```
kubectl apply -f .\Deploy\sample.microservice.order.yaml
kubectl apply -f .\Deploy\sample.microservice.reservation.yaml
kubectl apply -f .\Deploy\sample.microservice.reservationactor.
yaml
kubectl apply -f .\Deploy\sample.microservice.customization.
yaml
kubectl apply -f .\Deploy\sample.microservice.shipping.yaml
```

With the preceding commands, we applied the aforementioned changes to all our application deployments.

With the following command, we can verify that the Horizontal Pod Autoscalers for our Dapr application have been configured:

```
kubectl get hpa
NAME                              REFERENCE
TARGETS    MINPODS    MAXPODS    REPLICAS    AGE
customization-service-hpa         Deployment/customization-service
13%/50%    1          4          1           2m21s
order-service-hpa                 Deployment/order-service
15%/50%    1          4          1           2m28s
reservation-service-hpa           Deployment/reservation-service
14%/50%    1          4          1           2m25s
reservationactor-service-hpa      Deployment/reservationactor-
service    20%/50%    1          4            1          2m23s
shipping-service-hpa              Deployment/shipping-service
3%/50%     1          4          1           2m18s
```

A HPA analyzes the metrics of resources used by the pods in a deployment. Once it detects an increase in CPU usage that's beyond the configured threshold, it triggers an increase in replicas.

The load test we will set up in the next configuration will trigger this mechanism.

Load testing with Locust

Load testing is a practice in software development that's used to determine the performance of a complex system under load. This is generated by simulating the concurrent access of users. Load testing web resources, such as an API, usually requires multiple agents to be orchestrated, each with enough internet bandwidth and compute resources to simulate the activity of many users.

In our scenario, we plan to verify the performance and capabilities of our *Biscotti Brutti Ma Buoni* sample backend, implemented with Dapr and running on Kubernetes.

Locust is a popular open source load testing tool. It allows you to define a user's behavior with simple Python scripts and distribute these on as many **worker nodes** as needed, orchestrated by a **master node**. More information is available at `https://locust.io/`.

> **Important note**
>
> I learned about Locust from a GitHub repository (`https://github.com/yorek/locust-on-azure`) that was created by my colleague Davide Mauri, PM in the Azure SQL team at Microsoft.
> This repository offers deployment scripts that allow you to use Azure Container Instances as a compute option for Locust master and workers. I personally contributed to the repository with a virtual network integrated deployment option.

The **Locust on Azure** repository has already been copied to this chapter's base directory. You can clone it by using the following command:

```
PS C:\Repos\dapr-samples\chapter10> git clone https://github.com/yorek/locust-on-azure.git
```

Once the repository has been cloned, copy the ready-to-use Locust test:

```
PS C:\Repos\dapr-samples\chapter10> copy .\loadtest\locustfile.py .\locust-on-azure\locust
```

Let's open the `chapter10\locust-on-azure\locust\locustfile.py` file to examine the Locust test for our scenario:

```python
from locust import HttpUser, TaskSet, task, between
import random
import json
from datetime import datetime
import uuid
```

```
import string

... omitted ...

class APIUser(HttpUser):
    wait_time = between(0.1, 1)

    @task(50)
    def getbalance(self):
        SKU = RandomSKU()
        with self.client.get("/balance/%s" % SKU,
        name="balance", catch_response=True) as response:
            if (not(response.status_code == 201 or 200)):
                    response.failure("Error balance: %s" %
                    response.text)

    @task(1)
    def postorder(self):
        http_headers = {'content-type': 'application/json'}
        payload = RandomOrder()

        with self.client.post("/order", json=payload,
        headers=http_headers, name="order", catch_
        response=True) as response:
            if (not(response.status_code == 201 or 200)):
                response.failure("Error order: %s" % response.
                text)
```

From the preceding Python snippet, we can see a class arbitrarily named `APIUser`: Locust will use each class to represent user behavior. In our test, we have only one, which, with a delay between 100 ms and 1 second, as expressed by `wait_time = between(0.1, 1)`, executes the methods decorated with `@task`. There are two methods, each with a different weight: `getbalance`, for reading the balance of a product by its SKU, and `@task(50)`, which has a 50 times higher chance to be executed than `postorder`, a method used to simulate an order submission.

As we saw previously, a Locust test is a simple `.py` Python file. For further information on this, it is worth looking at the quickstart presented at `https://docs.locust.io/en/stable/quickstart.html`.

Now that we've looked at the Locust test definition and have a suitable example ready, we can launch it to assess the performance of our Dapr applications.

Load testing Dapr

Before we activate a more complex test infrastructure for Locust on Azure Container Instances, it is best to first check, and eventually debug, the Locust test locally. The following steps take us through preparing the data to enabling autoscaling on a running load test:

1. Preparing the data via port-forward

2. Testing Locust locally

3. Locust on Azure Container Instances

4. Configuring the Horizontal Pod Autoscaler

First, we need to make sure the data in our environment can support our scenario. This we'll do in the next section.

Preparing the data via port-forward

Before we launch the test, which is readily available at `chapter10\locust-on-azure\locust\locustfile.py`, let's focus on an aspect we oversaw: the SKU for the cookies is randomly composed from **cookie001** to **cookie999**, with the addition of the infamous **crazycookie**, the main actor (pun intended) of the saga from *Chapter 5, Publish and Subscribe*.

The code that's being used for our sample Dapr applications is extremely permissive: you could order an item with a negative balance without an issue. You can also add both validation and business logic to it, in case you are interested.

Nevertheless, all the `getbalance` test requests will fail since the items that have been created by these SKUs are unknown by the Dapr applications. We can prepare the data by launching the `C:\Repos\dapr-samples\chapter10\loader\generatedata.py` Python file.

There is nothing special in this data generator script, other than it relies on reaching `ReservationItemActor`, which is not exposed via an ingress controller, at the standard Dapr API URL of `http://locahost:5001/v1.0/actors/ReservationItemActor/{id}/method/AddReservation`, with `{id}` being the random cookie SKU.

In order to use the script, we need to use port-forwarding to locally map port 5001 to the Dapr sidecar port 3500 in any of the pods containing our Dapr applications in Kubernetes. With the following command, you can obtain the name of a pod in Dapr:

```
kubectl port-forward order-service-6c5f494bcb-qqs7g 5001:3500
```

With port-forwarding, we can gain access to a Dapr sidecar running inside Kubernetes. We can launch the C:\Repos\dapr-samples\chapter10\loader\ generatedata.py script from VS Code or a Windows terminal session with the following command:

```
PS C:\Repos\dapr-samples\chapter10\loader> python .\
generatedata.py
```

Once all the instances for the 1,000 ReservationItemActor have been created, we can proceed with the Locust tests.

Testing Locust locally

To launch the chapter10\locust-on-azure\locust\locustfile.py test file with Locust, use the following command:

```
PS C:\Repos\dapr-samples\chapter10\locust-on-azure\locust>
locust -H http://dapringresssdb.westeurope.cloudapp.azure.com
/bbmb
```

The -H parameter set the host address. Since the tests invoke /balance and /order, the host should contain the base path, including the domain name that's been defined for the ingress controller.

For our first run, which will tell us whether the tests are correct, let's simulate a few users with a slow spawning rate. If we encounter any unexpected exceptions, meaning that there's a bug in our test code, we can increase the number of users.

Let's ramp up the test to 1,000 users!

In the following screenshot, you can start to see why executing a load test from a single node it is not a good idea:

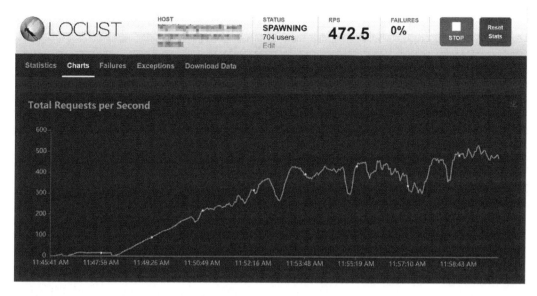

Figure 10.3 – Locust RPS encountering high CPU usage

In the preceding screenshot, you can see the Locust dashboard. It shows how the **requests per second** (**RPS**) have reached a plateau of 400 RPS and that they are not moving from there. From a Kubernetes perspective, I did not see any high CPU utilization.

Once I looked at the Windows terminal session running Locust, I saw the following output:

```
PS C:\Repos\dapr-samples\chapter10\locust-on-azure\locust>
locust -H http://<ingress>.<aks prefix>/bbmb
[2020-10-31 11:46:56,730] DB-SURFACEBOOK2/INFO/locust.main:
Starting web interface at http://0.0.0.0:8089 (accepting con
nections from all network interfaces)
[2020-10-31 11:46:56,746] DB-SURFACEBOOK2/INFO/locust.main:
Starting Locust 1.3.1
[2020-10-31 11:48:21,076] DB-SURFACEBOOK2/INFO/locust.runners:
Spawning 1000 users at the rate 1 users/s (0 users alread
y running)...
[2020-10-31 11:51:57,393] DB-SURFACEBOOK2/WARNING/root: CPU
usage above 90%! This may constrain your throughput and may
even give inconsistent response time measurements! See https://
```

```
docs.locust.io/en/stable/running-locust-distributed.html
for how to distribute the load over multiple CPU cores or
machines
```

I'm running Locust from my local development machine to check the quality of the tests. However, as reported in the output, I already encountered a CPU with high stress conditions.

Considering the high CPU usage warning, in conjunction with the time series shown in the preceding screenshot, this could well be a factor that's negatively impacting the validity of the overall test.

Now that we've stopped the load test, let's focus on the metrics presented by Locust:

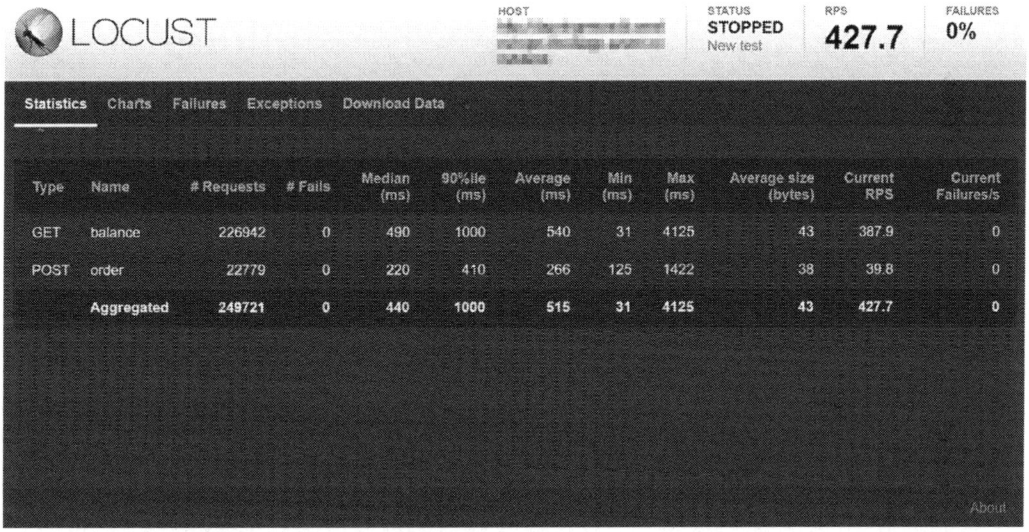

Figure 10.4 – Locust test statistics

In the preceding screenshot, you can appreciate the data presented by Locust on the **Statistics** pane, which is where the performance of each task is presented. This information, including exceptions and failures reports, are also available a CSV file that you can download.

Your experience may change, depending on the CPU and network bandwidth of the local machine you are using for Locust, as well as the network capacity of your site.

In this section, we learned how to write a Locust test, how to test it locally, how to interpret the Locust metrics, and, most importantly, why an Azure-based deployment of a Locust swarm is a good approach so that we have an effective load testing environment.

Locust on Azure Container Instances

The Locust on Azure implementation offered at `https://github.com/yorek/locust-on-azure` leverages the **Azure Container Instances** (**ACI**) resource to execute Locust in distributed mode, along with master and worker nodes.

While AKS offers containers orchestrated by Kubernetes, ACI allows us to execute individual containers without the need for an orchestrator.

The following diagram shows how the solution is composed:

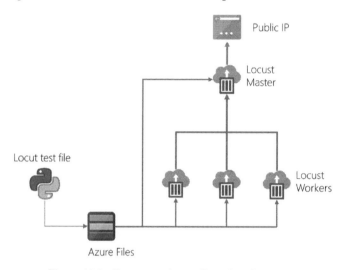

Figure 10.5 – Locust on Azure Container Instances

The template is activated by executing the `\locust-on-azure\azure-deploy.sh` script, which can be found in this chapter's base directory. The script uploads the Python files present in the `\locust-on-azure\locust` directory to a newly created Azure Files storage. This storage option in Azure is mounted on all Azure Container Instances. Finally, Locust is activated on the ACI, with the worker nodes interacting with the master node. This is the one exposing the Locust portal to the users, as shown in the preceding diagram.

Locust on Azure is a shell script; therefore, we need to shift to Windows Subsystem for Linux, as described in the *Technical requirements* section. We also need to access our Azure subscription from this context with `az login`. Once we've done this, we can launch the `azure-deploy.sh` script:

```
master@DB-SURFACEBOOK2:/c/Repos/dapr-samples/chapter10/locust-
on-azure$ ./azure-deploy.sh
Environment file not detected.
Please configure values for your environment in the created
```

```
.env file and run the script again.
TEST_CLIENTS: Number of locust client to create
USERS_PER_CLIENT: Number of users that each locust client will
simulate
SPAWN_RATE: How many new users will be created per second per
locust client
HOST: REST Endpoint to test
RESOURCE_GROUP: Resource group where Locust will be deployed
AZURE_STORAGE_ACCOUNT: Storage account name that will be
created to host the locust file
```

As described in the first execution, we need to specify a few variables in order to describe the destination environment. Once we've specified those in the .env files in the same \locust-on-azure\locust directory, the setup will be complete and successfully deploying the resources to Azure:

```
master@DB-SURFACEBOOK2:/c/Repos/dapr-samples/chapter10/locust-
on-azure$ ./azure-deploy.sh
loading from .env
starting
creating storage account: daprlocustsharedstorage
retrieving storage connection string
creating file share
uploading simulator scripts
uploading /c/Repos/dapr-samples/chapter10/locust-on-azure/
locust/locustfile.py
Finished[#######################################]
100.0000%
deploying locust (10 clients)...
locust: endpoint: http://<omitted>:8089
locust: starting ...
locust: users: 1000, spawn rate: 10
```

Once we've deployed the script, we receive the endpoint of our Locust portal.

Now that we have a proper testing platform for a Locust swarm running on Azure, unbridled from the CPU and bandwidth constraints of a single workstation, we are ready to launch a new test.

Configuring the Horizontal Pod Autoscaler

In this chapter, we learned how a Horizontal Pod Autoscaler operates. Now, it is time to see it in action.

Let's launch the Locust test from the portal. This time, it can be reached at the public IP of the master ACI, as printed in the output shown in the previous section.

Since we are aiming to apply a load of 1,000 concurrent users to our API, let's examine the behavior of the HPA with the `kubectl get hpa -w` command while the Locust swarm starts executing requests:

```
PS C:\Repos\dapr-samples\chapter10> kubectl get hpa -w
NAME                                TARGETS      REPLICAS    AGE
customization-service-hpa           78%/50%      1           14m
order-service-hpa                   139%/50%     1           14m
reservation-service-hpa             185%/50%     4           14m
reservationactor-service-hpa        147%/50%     1           14m
shipping-service-hpa                2%/50%       1           14m
reservation-service-hpa             255%/50%     1           14m
customization-service-hpa           78%/50%      2           14m
order-service-hpa                   139%/50%     3           15m
reservationactor-service-hpa        142%/50%     4           14m
reservation-service-hpa             255%/50%     4           15m
customization-service-hpa           10%/50%      2           15m
order-service-hpa                   29%/50%      3           15m
reservationactor-service-hpa        66%/50%      8           15m
shipping-service-hpa                2%/50%       1           15m
reservation-service-hpa             142%/50%     8           15m
reservationactor-service-hpa        66%/50%      10          15m
reservation-service-hpa             142%/50%     10          15m
```

A few columns have been removed from the preceding output to evidence the growth in replicas enforced by the HPAs. This was triggered by an increase in CPU usage by the `reservation-service` and `reservationactor-service` applications. These Dapr applications perform most of the operations in the overall solution, so this behavior was expected.

Let's examine the same data, but plotted on a chart:

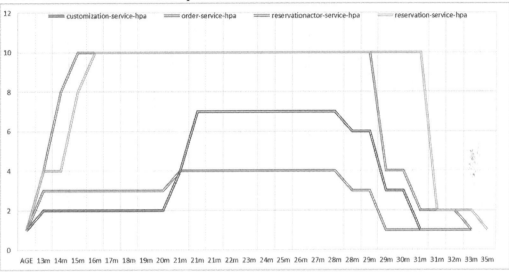

Figure 10.6 – Horizontal Pod Autoscaler scaling up and down

As we can see, the HPA for the `reservation-service` and `reservationactor-service` applications scaled up quickly to 10 pod instances and kept at the maximum limit imposed by the HPA for the duration of the test. Once they had done this, they scaled down during the cooling period to the minimum number of pods; that is, 1:

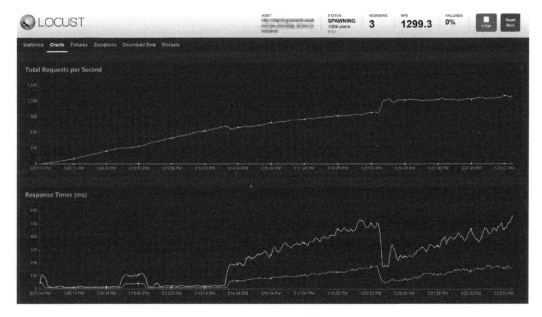

Figure 10.7 – Locust load test

There are several other aspects to account for during a load test: the impact on the Dapr state store and publish/subscribe is extremely relevant. In the preceding screenshot, we can see a few spikes in the response time that should be investigated.

By looking at the Locust portal, we can see that setting a higher number of pods could have had a positive impact.

If our load test was aiming to allow 1,000 concurrent users to interact with our Dapr application's API, with an end-to-end response time of about half a second, having nearly 1,200 requests per second could be a satisfactory result.

Before we complete our load testing journey, let's consider another autoscaling option.

Autoscaling with KEDA

So far, we've learned that the Horizontal Pod Autoscaler is triggered by the CPU and memory metrics of the pods in a deployment.

Kubernetes-based Event-Driven Autoscaling (KEDA) is a **Cloud Native Computing Foundation** (**CNCF**) project with the objective of extending the capabilities of the Kubernetes HPA so that it reacts to the metrics of resources that are external to the Kubernetes cluster.

You can learn more about KEDA (`https://keda.sh/`) in the context of Dapr at `https://docs.dapr.io/developing-applications/integrations/autoscale-keda/`.

Considering the vast adoption of the publish/subscribe Dapr building block in our example, it would be smart to increase (and decrease) the number of pods based on the messages accumulating in the underlying messaging system, which is Azure Service Bus in our case. If the number of enqueued messages grows, we could add more pods so that Dapr dequeues the messages and our ASP.NET Core code processes the requests.

In more general terms, reacting to the metrics of the incoming messages is useful if we wish to anticipate a load other than the stress that occurs in processing.

KEDA offers scalers for most of the publish/subscribe components supported by Dapr, which makes it a powerful tool at our disposal.

Summary

In this chapter, we learned how to scale the Kubernetes resources of our Dapr applications with the deployment configuration, as well as how to automatically adapt the number of replicas to CPU and memory usage with the Horizontal Pod Autoscaler.

The concepts we explored in this chapter gave us a more solid approach to testing Dapr applications under specific conditions: is our overall solution, starting with the nodes of the Kubernetes cluster, including the database (state store) and message bus (publish/subscribe), capable of sustaining a specific load?

Even if we had to venture outside of the land of C# and .NET Core to leverage Locust, I think the advantages of learning a popular, developer oriented, load testing framework justifies the effort. Python is also supported in Dapr with SDK for services and actors, so maybe this could be the next stage of our learning experience with Dapr?

I hope you enjoyed this Dapr learning experience. This was a journey which started with the basics of Dapr and ended with load testing a solution powered by Dapr and deployed on Kubernetes.

Appendix: Microservices Architectures with Dapr

In this chapter, I intend to discuss the relevance of microservices architectures to building modern applications, and to explore how Dapr, as a runtime, can make this cultural shift way easier to adopt in order to achieve the many advantages that come with it. Learning why and how microservices are beneficial will help you in making better use of Dapr too.

We're going to cover the following main topics:

- Discovering microservices
- Adopting microservices patterns
- Building an e-commerce architecture
- Building microservices with Dapr

We'll start by exploring the basic concepts of microservices architectures' design.

Discovering microservices

There is an endless collection of books, papers, and blog posts that excellently describe and analyze the microservice-style architecture. The objective of this chapter is to present to you with the advantages and challenges of using a microservices architecture, to find out how Dapr can help us create new applications based on it.

The nemesis of a microservices architecture is the monolith: no one would ever admit they built or are still working on one. But most of us, in the development industry, spent many years working on monolith applications. In a monolith, as the name implies, all the business capabilities or features are condensed in a single application, probably layered between the UI, server and database but nevertheless not designed in a modular or distributed fashion.

In a microservice architecture, the services designed to support business capabilities are most likely to communicate with open protocols such as HTTP and gRPC, are built and released via automation, can be independently deployed and each microservice's team can adopt the language and technology stack best fits their needs.

As microservices are an evolution of **Service Oriented Architecture (SOA)**, let me briefly summarize the overall architectural concepts we are dealing with in the following sections:

- Service
- Autonomy
- Automated deployment
- Bounded context
- Loose coupling
- Event-driven architecture
- Observability
- Sustainability

We will look at these individually in the following sections. Let's start by exploring the core concept of a service.

Service

A service is a logical representation of a process capable of fulfilling a business activity: to sell a product to a potential customer, to support a customer in fixing an issue with the product, and so on.

A service exposes an **Application Programming Interface (API)** that regulates how the interaction with the service can happen.

It is very likely that the API will be defined as a REST API over HTTP, as most of the developer audience would expect in today's world, but the concept is not restricted to a specific implementation detail. As an example, gRPC is also a popular choice for exposing a service.

From the client's perspective, there is no interest in being, or needing to be aware of the internal mechanisms of the service. What matters to the client is the API contract, its stability over time, and the Service Level Agreement that indicates the objectives of availability and performance the service promises to uphold, as well as the reparations in case it is not able to keep those promises.

Autonomy

A microservice should be autonomous in reaching its objective declared via the API, regardless of its dependencies toward other services. Autonomy applies to operations and evolution as well.

In order to gain more autonomy, the service should limit the need to coordinate with dependent services: the more dependencies a service has, the more difficult it will be to respect the desired availability and to evolve, as changes to other services will impact your service over time.

Let's look at an example: your application has two microservices, each relying on a common portion of code. As you identify this common ground, a case for a new microservice is made by separating the common portion of code into a new service. Does this make any sense? Not from my perspective: consider instead refactoring the common code as a library and distributing it via NuGet, the package manager, so that the two microservices are free to control which version they use and when to update it.

Is this common portion of code the starting point of a new business capability that will grow over time? This would shed a different light on the scenario, which is more favorable for a third microservice that will introduce more coordination.

There should be a very good reason to add coordination to a dependent service, since having others depend on your microservice is a responsibility not to be taken lightly.

Automated deployment

By introducing microservices, you will tend to have more independently deployable units of code (which I see as a benefit) for several reasons. For example, different teams may be working on separate projects. Whatever the reason, you will need to adopt Continuous Deployment practices and tools to perform these operations in an automated fashion. Otherwise, if performed manually, the build and deployment process of microservices could be much more time-consuming than those of a monolith application.

Bounded context

Bounded context is a pattern that originated in the domain-driven design space. The unified model of an enterprise/large application tends to grow significantly large, and therefore it becomes intrinsically difficult to manage, especially over time. Splitting the complex model into smaller, more independent but integrated models, each with a coherent purpose, can be a solution.

As an example, an e-commerce application might be difficult to manage as a single model. Can we agree that separating the context of sales from after-sales (support, products return, and complaints handling) might be a good, simplified approach?

The *micro* in microservices suggests the idea of *small*, but according to which measure? Is it the number of classes? The portable executable size as a file? The overall number of libraries?

In my opinion the word *micro* does not help to clarify the concept, while bounded context is far more useful to indicate that a microservice should take care of a single part of the application: the reduced size of a microservice compared to a monolith is often a byproduct of this.

Loose coupling

Directly from the SOA space, the interactions between two services should be as loosely coupled as possible: if you reach this goal, you could deploy a service without impacting others.

This goal can be reached by implementing patterns that favor an indirect interaction (publish-subscribe) over a direct request-reply. While it's not easy to keep services loosely coupled, this might prove an insurmountable task, hence a further analysis should verify whether the services (or microservices) in scope are meant to be kept separate or should be combined instead.

If this seems familiar to the concept of autonomy, you are right: as a matter of fact, the looser you couple two microservices, the more autonomous they are.

Event-driven architecture

Event-driven is an architectural pattern in which events, such as changes in the state or facts, are produced for others, unknown to the producer, to be noticed and eventually consumed. For example, a new sale being launched, or the quantity of a product reaching 0 and therefore being out of stock, are two types of events.

With this pattern, a service is triggered not by a direct invocation, but by the detection of a message representing the event. Inherently, each of the parties, the producer and the consumer, operates at a scale and speed that fit their own objectives, not interfering with each other.

In order to build an event driven architecture, you will likely leverage a message bus to handle the complexity of exchanging messages.

Observability

A microservice architecture brings many more moving parts into play, being deployed more frequently, probably in a greater number of instances, over many hosts. It is therefore paramount to gain full visibility of the status and behavior of each microservice instance, each point of coordination, and each component of the underlying platform/runtime, making it easy for both the operators' and developers' audiences to gain an easily readable and actionable intelligence from this vast group of information.

In contrast to our usual experiences, counting on accessing the logs from all the nodes will not help much; having a synthetic probe result letting you know the microservice is up is surely useful, but it won't tell you as much as knowing that the microservice is demonstrating its ability to consistently perform its business capability over time. What you want to achieve is having full traceability for each request as it crosses all boundaries between microservices and the underlying stores and services.

Sustainability

Given the current historical context as we face a climate crisis with rapidly increasing temperature, there is much interest in sustainable operations, and lately, I have experienced the growth of a community working toward sustainable software engineering.

Sustainable Software Engineering is a new discipline combining climate science with software architecture – the way electricity is generated with how data centers and hardware are designed. See more about this at `https://principles.green`.

The overall picture is that developers, software analysts, and even application owners should take into account the carbon impact of their software, and all the possible ways to reduce it or at least adapt it to the conditions of the underlying energy offering. The perfect example of this discipline is the low carbon Kubernetes scheduler (the whitepaper is available at `http://ceur-ws.org/Vol-2382/ICT4S2019_paper_28.pdf`), which helps developers move their application's containers according to the lowest carbon impact of the current location. I think Dapr also has the ability to influence this movement. This is because it makes microservice applications so much easier to write and handle–adding the sustainability option should not be a huge effort–and besides, architecting a software to not waste resources should be in our best interest anyway.

As we share a common understanding of the core concepts of a microservice architecture, let's see the benefits its adoption gives us.

Adopting microservices patterns

Which benefits does a microservice architecture bring to an application? Why should we move from monoliths to microservices?

Considering the concepts described so far, I think the following might be a good list of improvements you can achieve by adopting a microservice architecture:

- **Evolution**: It is common to have several smaller teams, each working with the tools, the languages, and platforms best matching their objectives: by defining a simpler and smaller (bounded) context for the application, there are far better chances that the evolution and growth of it will be faster, more reliable, and have a better business impact.

- **Flexibility**: By becoming as autonomous as possible, by interacting with others in a loosely coupled manner, the microservice will gain many opportunities otherwise impossible for a monolithic architecture: changing the persistence layer, adopting a new library, or even switching to a different technology stack now become a possibility. As long as there is no impact on other microservices, each team is free to choose its own innovation path.

- **Reliability**: Code quality will not improve by itself just because it is in a microservice, but having a smaller scope and being able to deploy it individually makes it easier to test it in an automated fashion, and will have increased reliability as a byproduct.

- **Scale**: Microservices enable you to deploy as many instances you need, dynamically increasing and reducing (scale-out and -in) the amount of resources, and even independently choosing the right resource, such as a specific database or a virtual machine type (scale-up and -down), equipped with a specific CPU your code can better leverage. These newly acquired abilities enable your application to achieve a much higher throughput rate, more efficiently than with other approaches.

> **Important note**
>
> With merit to scale, microservices are often cited as the default architecture for application landing on Kubernetes, because of its ability to scale and coordinate resources.
>
> Kubernetes is a good choice for hosting microservice architectures, as could a **Function as a Service (FaaS)** offering like Azure Functions be, to some degree.
>
> In FaaS the focus is only on the application code, with a greater abstraction from the infrastructure layer than with a deployment based on containers.
>
> The point of attention is just to keep the subjects separate; Kubernetes can sometimes be an appropriate hosting platform for monolith applications condensed into a single pod as well.

All the benefits a microservice architecture brings to the application translate to an advantage for your product in the market against the competition.

This book is focused on .NET Core, which we all deeply love, but it will probably not be the only language used by your application. If your application needs to leverage machine learning, whether for existing models or to train new ones, these are disciplines in which the audience is more comfortable with Python, just to start with the obvious. Therefore, being able to fully leverage the job market, because your architecture paradigm allows you to choose the best technology for the task, can be a strategic advantage to not underestimate.

It is a good exercise to ask ourselves the following question: *should we always adopt microservices?*

Microservice architectures are the distilled outcome of endless improvements in the way software is designed and built, therefore it's up to us, architects, and developers, to adopt the latest and best in our daily jobs.

Nevertheless, I think every technology should be adopted only if it brings a net benefit.

If there is only a team (of a few members) working on the application, splitting a monolith into microservices will not make it easier for the very same team to cope with the burden of more projects, more complex dependencies, nor separate CD pipelines, just to name a few.

At infinite resources, a monolith application might be able to scale to meet your goal by adding new instances of your host of choice, a virtual machine for instance. As long as more powerful virtual machines become available, your monolith application would always have room for growth.

The scale for which microservices emerged as a winning architecture might be way beyond your needs, but on the other hand, a monolith was not built to deal with the complexity of managing updates and coordination over too many hosts and instances.

If the team did not reach proper maturity on automated testing and CI/CD (namely, the overall DevOps culture) it might be a significant challenge to adopt microservices and handle all the above-mentioned issues at the same time. Nevertheless, if time and resources are in your favor, you can try to kill two birds with one stone.

Finally, it might become difficult to identify clear context boundaries in your applications, maybe because it fulfills a very specific task and not much more. In these cases, there might not be a clear benefit in further splitting it, needlessly, into microservices. Nevertheless, adopting the same patterns and aiming for the same goals of microservice architectures might help you in the long run.

Building an e-commerce architecture

The objective of this book is to illustrate how Dapr can support your job, as a developer and architect, in creating an application adopting a microservice architecture. I think it helps to discuss a hypothetical scenario over the course of the chapters to see how each feature can be introduced: I considered a scenario we all experience once or more in our daily lives, mostly as consumers, sometimes as creators, building an e-commerce site.

An e-commerce site must support many capabilities: exposing a catalog and making it browsable, having a price model that can be influenced by a promotion engine, managing a shopping cart, collecting customer information, processing orders, fulfilling the orders, and coordinating the shipment, just to name a few.

Throughout the book we composed a sample solution, using the fictional e-commerce site named *Biscotti Brutti Ma Buoni*. This site specializes in the production and customization of cookies: most of their customers don't buy the plain cookies' packaging, but order customized versions for special occasions. *Biscotti Brutti Ma Buoni* is widely known for their ability to digitally print complex multilayer scenes on a cookie.

Starting with this fictional sample of e-commerce, we will explore the context of its components that we want to include as microservices in our solution.

Bounded contexts

As we were not able to interview the business and domain expert of the fictional e-commerce site, I briefly ask for your suspension of disbelief, as if you were watching a play. Let's agree we identified several bounded contexts:

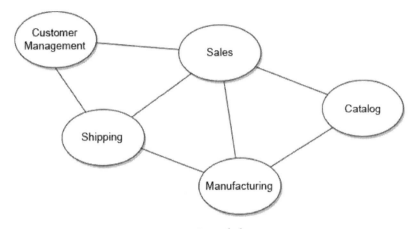

Figure A.1 – Bounded contexts

Starting with the *Figure A.1*, let's focus our attention on a few of these contexts:

- **Sales:** Most sold items are made on-demand and might require customization; therefore, sales orders tend to be accepted only if the manufacturing process is active. The stock is relevant during the manufacturing process: if for any reason a product line is temporarily unavailable because a particular ingredient is missing or a piece of equipment had a fault, the order might be put on hold, or cancelled, and the item would become unavailable in the front store.

- **Manufacturing**: Luckily for *Biscotti Brutti Ma Buoni* most of the items offered for sale are made from the same dough, therefore planning for the main ingredients is simple. Customization is more complex as colorants and other ingredients for icing are much more diverse. The request to manufacture the final item is guided by the actual sale, but the provisioning of ingredients is driven by a machine learning model that takes into account seasonal and short-term sales. Manufacturing also encompasses the customization of the cookie.

- **Shipping**: While shipping is important to all e-commerce sites, as nowadays customers are used to immediate delivery, for perishable and delicate goods the order fulfillment demands maximum care.

To facilitate the exploration of Dapr, the connection between the bounded contexts will prefer a coordination via service invocation and pub/sub instead of data duplication or any other approach.

An example – sales microservices

As an example, let's suppose the further analysis of the sales bounded context is going to express the following microservices:

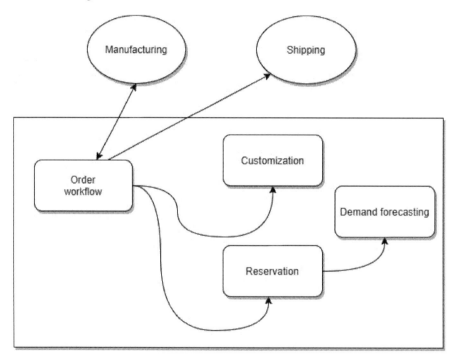

Figure A.2 – Sales bounded context

As we can see from *Figure A.2,* a sales order triggers the preparation workflow via a loosely coupled interaction. The **Reservation** service will also be informed by consuming events on the order status update. Once the order preparation workflow successfully completes, it will trigger **Shipping** as the next step.

Building microservices with Dapr

How can Dapr help us build this e-commerce application by adopting a microservices architecture?

In this section, we will learn the specific benefits Dapr brings for the characteristics of a microservice architecture. Let's start by exploring loosely coupled microservices.

Loosely coupled microservices

With pub/sub in Dapr we can achieve two objectives. Not only does Dapr make it transparent to use any of the supported messaging systems, such as Redis, RabbitMQ, Azure Service Bus, and Azure Event Hub, it also provides all the plumbing code responsible for handling the message operations, ensuring at-least-once delivery.

Two microservices, signaling each other an event via pub/sub, can coordinate via a loosely coupled connection. If the consumer is experiencing a temporary issue, the information sent by the producer will stay safely in the messaging subsystem of choice, waiting for the consumer to come back and get it.

Autonomous microservices

A service with Dapr can be invoked by just specifying an application identifier: it is then Dapr's responsibility to discover where the service is running in the hosted environment (most likely Kubernetes), how to reach it, and how to handle its request/response via a secure communication channel.

If the invoked service, over time, evolves to adopt a different set of libraries, to change the data layer or the data storage itself, then with Dapr it will appear and operate just the same.

Observable microservices

The microservices identified in the manufacturing bounded context interact with each other and with other bounded contexts as well, communicating between many different hosting environments: the nodes and pods of Kubernetes and the state stores, the messaging systems, and so on.

It soon becomes clear that while a collection of logs from the Kubernetes infrastructure is helpful, what is much more needed is a distributed tracing of each activity as its processing flows from one step to the next, from one microservice to the other, by sharing the common context of the customer journey.

Scalable microservices

Dapr promotes the usage of Kubernetes as the hosting platform of your microservices, enabling dynamic and rapid scaling of each one independently on as many resources, pods, and nodes as needed.

Over this book's chapters we learned how easy it is, with Dapr, to create microservices: from this perspective, Dapr enables the architects and developers to consider only the bounded context and microservices analysis to define the implementation details of the architecture. Unnecessary proliferation of microservices is to be avoided and Dapr will not push your architecture toward more microservices or less, but it will significantly reduce the initial effort needed.

Event driven microservices

An event driven architecture can be achieved in many ways: as an example, I can have a loop in my code that monitors the messaging or external subsystems, via a long polling approach, for new events.

In this scenario I would be responsible for keeping the process active, whether I rely on a PaaS or IaaS hosting environment: my code could leverage a library to spare me from the inner details of the message system, nevertheless I am still influenced by the process and host recycling as I have to keep listening for events. Only at the end of this complex chain of elements will I have the value-added code with my logic.

It is a subtle but important difference: not having a library but counting on a runtime, designed to operate in complex conditions, in an environment such as Kubernetes, capable of fast recovery. This reduces the code under my responsibility to just the message handling logic and is a tremendous advantage offered by Dapr.

Stateless microservices

A stateless microservice is easier to distribute over as many instances as needed, has a faster life cycle, and is more solid in handling faults and conditions of error.

Nevertheless, many – if not most – of the microservices we create need to manage a state, whether it is used to support the processing of a request or it represents the core data the code is handling.

By managing state as a service, with pluggable interchangeable components, Dapr makes any microservice practically a stateless microservice. With the reliable state API provided by Dapr, the complexity of managing state by taking concurrency and consistency into account is lifted from the service code.

Summary

In conclusion, the reason why Dapr has an immediate appeal to cloud-native developers is its ability to provide flexibility and simplicity in a very complex environment. As a fellow Microsoft colleague often tells us, only ten years ago an entire developer's career could be built on what today is just a simple scaling slider.

This is the future of development, and in addition to the cloud-native tools, Dapr also offers the chance to bring together all the possible combinations of legacy applications and programming languages, so that a complete refactoring is no longer the only modernization option.

Other Books You May Enjoy

If you enjoyed this book, you may be interested in these other books by Packt:

C# 9 and .NET 5 – Modern Cross-Platform Development - Fifth Edition

Mark J. Price

ISBN: 978-1-80056-810-5

- Build your own types with object-oriented programming

- Query and manipulate data using LINQ

- Build websites and services using ASP.NET Core 5

- Create intelligent apps using machine learning

- Use Entity Framework Core and work with relational databases

- Discover Windows app development using the Universal Windows Platform and XAML

- Build rich web experiences using the Blazor framework

- Build mobile applications for iOS and Android using Xamarin.Forms

Learn C# Programming

Marius Bancila, Raffaele Rialdi, Ankit Sharma

ISBN: 978-178980-586-4

- Get to grips with all the new features of C# 8

- Discover how to use attributes and reflection to build extendable applications

- Utilize LINQ to uniformly query various sources of data

- Use files and streams and serialize data to JSON and XML

- Write asynchronous code with the async-await pattern

- Employ .NET Core tools to create, compile, and publish your applications

- Create unit tests with Visual Studio and the Microsoft unit testing frameworks

Leave a review - let other readers know what you think

Please share your thoughts on this book with others by leaving a review on the site that you bought it from. If you purchased the book from Amazon, please leave us an honest review on this book's Amazon page. This is vital so that other potential readers can see and use your unbiased opinion to make purchasing decisions, we can understand what our customers think about our products, and our authors can see your feedback on the title that they have worked with Packt to create. It will only take a few minutes of your time, but is valuable to other potential customers, our authors, and Packt. Thank you!

Index

Symbols

A

Made in the USA
Las Vegas, NV
25 June 2021

25418925R00144